Christ
Incognito

Imagining,
Encountering,
Embracing and
Embodying His Love

DOUG STEVENS

FOREWARD BY LORI STANLEY ROELEVELD

Author of *The Art of Hard Conversations* and *Running From a Crazy Man*

THE
RENEWAL
PROJECT INC.

Published by The Renewal Project • Austin, TX U.S.A.

This book is a collection of raves, riffs and reflections, an open-ended exploration transporting us here and there (and everywhere) in search of the most intriguing and compelling personality in all of human history. Are you ready to ride?

Visit radicalaffirmationist.com

Dedicated to those who are on a serious search for the
Christ of history, the Christ at-large in our world,
the Christ who has come near in his desire to do us good.

Dedicated to those who have given up on such a search
but are nevertheless pursued by the Christ who loves
unconditionally and indiscriminately.

Dedicated to those who are walking with Christ in a
delightful and dangerous world, determined to live as
faithful followers who reflect his justice and mercy.

Christ Incognito

There is something inside us that longs for something more. *Is that all there is?* we ask wistfully, insistently—with a hint of hope and a trace of sorrow. The object of our desire might be vague or vivid. *I still haven't found what I'm looking for*, we lament...and keep on searching, avidly, even recklessly. Or, we give up and settle. Leaving an underlying sadness that is only incompletely suppressed.

ENCOUNTERING

Out of nowhere and without warning, it seems, a moment out of the ordinary, an epiphany interrupts our routines. Something or someone unexplainable but almost irresistible shows up. Hope ignites—and fear cautions us. What is this? Who is this?! We have to find out—or we turn away feeling unworthy or untrusting. But left wondering, what did we miss?

EMBRACING

This is risky. This invitation to embrace...is it genuine, is it safe, is it sustainable in a complicated, ever-changing world? We want nothing more than to believe—but is it true (am I the beloved?!), and will the embrace comfort us (my desperate need!) and strengthen us (my fondest wish!)—or expose us, shame us, smother us so we cannot breathe?

EMBODYING

If and when we discover that this embrace is in reality a reunion with God—can we, will we, live in alignment with the enabling impulse of this effusive love? Don't stop now! we tell ourselves. This is just the beginning. Everyone is on such a journey, even if they have been waylaid. God's love must be demonstrated in real time in real life by real people in real relationships.

LOVE

Love melts resistance, instigates faith, forgives offenses, carries burdens, gives itself away...is willing to wait for the fulfillment of the hope that motivates love to persevere with its last breath, sacrificing its last drop of blood, pouring out its whole heart.

Contents

Foreword   xii

Preview   xv

PART ONE: HIDING IN PLAIN SIGHT   1

God is Not   3

Episode One: The Radical Affirmationist   5

Amazing Grace   15

Episode Two: The Wrath of God   17

Episode Three: The Davio Factor   23

Nature vs. Grace   35

Found   37

Episode Four: The Logic of Love   39

PART TWO: AT THE END OF OURSELVES   69

It's a Cold and It's a Broken Hallelujah   71

Episode Five: Bloodbath   73

Your Sins   87

Episode Six: Powerful Parables   89

Episode Seven: The End of Religion   99

Episode Eight: Life's Secret Sauce   109

PART THREE: NO EYE HAS SEEN   137

Episode Nine: Rumors of a Resurrection   139

Episode Ten: Spirited Away   147

Episode Eleven: Into the Fire   161

Episode Twelve: Sabbath Rhythm   177

No One Saw This Coming   189

Christ Revealed   191

Afterword   199

Bibliography   207

Foreword

Here's what I love about Doug—and the fever I caught from him when he was my college professor—he adores the mystery of Jesus. The mystery of God made flesh in Jesus is what keeps our faith fresh even after decades of following Him. God requires a manna-driven faith that rots when we try to box it, hoard it, and store it on a shelf. We must gather it and use all we gather every day, reaching the night empty, needing a refill upon waking.

Christ Incognito reignites the power of being children amazed at the master of anything—master magician, musician, scientist, artist or athlete. Rather than formulas and prescriptions, Doug reminds us to follow Jesus with our eyes wide and our jaws dropped, and if that's not our experience to seek until we find the genuine article, not some stale carob version of the rich, dark chocolate adventure of relating to the Living God.

The mystery of God is not a mystery to be solved like a set of missing keys or a puzzle with limited pieces or a crime. The mystery of God is a mystery to be explored like the universe, the seven seas, the love of a beautiful human, or the wonder of a prodigy who produces art or music or mathematical equations we haven't even begun to imagine.

Whether you've been at this Jesus-following for a lifetime or aren't even sure He exists, *Christ Incognito* will give voice to that hunger you've been suppressing – tamping down with quick fixes that only quiet it but never satisfy. We are all famished for the God who creates—for the excitement, adventure, light, and life. For the God who smiles. The God who says Yes. The God whose anger is constructive and corrective and just. The God who persists, pursues, and prevails. The God we're designed to recognize because meeting Him is like coming home. The God we have no struggle to share because He escapes from us like holy laughter, like a deep sigh after a satisfying meal, like a story around a blazing fire, like a melody we cannot help but hum, like a match we strike in the dark.

I won't hold you back a moment longer. You're already itching for the adventure, aren't you? Follow Doug, now, as he takes you back to where you think you've never been but always longed to return—to the very heart of the very living God.

> —**Lori Stanley Roeleveld,** Jesus-lover, speaker, disturber of hobbits, and author of *Running from a Crazy Man (and other adventures traveling with Jesus)* and *The Art of Hard Conversations: Biblical Tools for the Tough Talks that Matter.* **www.loriroeleveld.com**

Preview

Who is your audience for this book? *Everyone*, is my answer, which sounds like wishful thinking even as I write this sentence. The first word in the title will immediately resonate with a Christian audience... and (maybe) turn away anyone irreligious, anyone not identifying themselves as a believer. The second word will likely confuse and perhaps provoke those who consider themselves Christians...and (possibly) intrigue people who have opted out of that tradition.

It does seem strange to try to put the two words together. The first, a name that attracts or repels, inspires or inflames, sometimes all at the same time. The second, a Latin word that deepens the mystery. Indicating that this person is "not known" or even "not knowable." Elusive, at best.

Christ *Incognito*. Suggesting that he is hidden, though a central figure in history—that his appearance among us, and the significance of his life might be missed. Or, is no longer relevant except as an historical curiosity, a catalogue of wonderful but unreachable ideals, or merely as a relic of superstition.

Another Latin term reminds us that there is a very large and vexing question waiting in the wings. *Deus Absconditus* is the view that God exists—but is absent, hidden away somewhere, and indifferent toward his creation. God left.

Does *Christ Incognito* imply *Deus Absconditus*? Is there nothing to it, after all? Are we all alone, fending for ourselves, doing the best we can in a world out of control, in a universe without meaning—except what we in our desperation attribute to it?

In the Greek language he is called *Christ*. The Jews call him *Messiah*. As do Muslims, with some modification, following the lead of the earlier Hebrew and Christian Testaments. Both words mean "the anointed one." Anointed—authorized by God, central in God's plan, and dispatched to intervene—to rescue the world from rampant evil, to deliver it from the consequences of grievous wrongdoing, to save it from itself and to restore humankind completely.

His followers call him Savior and Lord and by his given name, Jesus. They believe in the scandalous notion that Christ Incognito was God Incarnate. That Jesus the Christ was born into our world in a particular place (as a Mediterranean Jew) at a particular time (at the apogee of Roman dominance) and without privilege—identifying with the most marginalized of humanity, daring to express truth and grace without compromise, to the extreme of selflessness and sacrifice in order to enact God's revolutionary plan for renewing all of creation.

Those who may admire him but not accept the lofty claims made about him, sometimes appropriate the term Christ to universalize it and disaffiliate it from organized religion, turning it into an honored but impersonal principle for branding esoteric spiritual techniques.

Most people admire him...and wonder about him. He is, after all, Christ Incognito. But how to categorize him and where to find him, how to engage him and how to live differently if and when we do?

This is what I want to propose. Suspend your doubts and defer your questions for a season of fresh discovery. Or bring them with you. There is a breathtaking adventure that awaits. It is not for the faint of heart. Well, actually, it is for them, too. It's for all of us.

If Jesus was the Christ, and if he is alive and active as the New Testament affirms and generations of followers have reportedly discovered, then this search will be worth all the investigation, patience and reflection it takes. It's certainly one rumor that should be tracked down before we give up on the possibility of a loving purpose powerfully at work in our world.

A confession and disclaimer. I write from experience, as an eyewitness, as a student of this movement, and as a disciple who has frequently failed to live up to my faith. I write as a skeptic hardwired to reject extravagant claims about anything. But I'm not a cynic, most of the time. I try to be open-minded and want to be open-hearted. I don't want to miss what I cannot yet fully understand or explain.

I am determined not to be limited or held captive by any ideology, dogma, party line, denominational anomaly, or by what is trending. I don't want to fly blind or take foolish risks—but will if I must, if this ultimate and often unconventional exploration requires it.

It's much more interesting, definitely more stimulating, and certainly more enjoyable to venture with others into the great unknown. So, I appreciate your sharing this journey with me, if you will. In your own way, at your own pace, and for your own reasons, of course.

I hope that someone will email their feedback, impressions, complaints and breakthroughs along the way. This is not an academic exercise but an experience fraught with danger (especially to our egos), loaded with emotion (if we allow ourselves to feel it), riddled with assumptions (many inherited, many unacknowledged), and peppered with surprises...if taken seriously and not prematurely foreclosed. Inciting dialogue and further progress. And, if our hopes materialize, some sort of Connection.

Christ, where are you? Where are you when we most need you?!

— Doug Stevens
Austin TX
doug@radicalaffirmationist.com
December, 2019

Desolate

When I was lost at sea
When I'm no longer me
Were you asleep?
Did you forget?
Or have we never even met?
I've heard that only you can set us free

On a search for God knows what
I keep running in this rut
That leaves me empty
Always craving
Wondering if I'm worth saving
Losing hope is always the unkindest cut

Where were you when I was down?
Where are you, are you around?
Can you explain?
Can you please teach me?
Will your wisdom someday reach me?
Can you hear me or does doubt blot out the sound?

I'll try again, I'm not sure why
I don't think I'll ever fly
At most to wish
I just exist
Instead of living I subsist
Yet I'm still here, I can't choke back this desolate cry

PART ONE

Hiding In Plain Sight

CHRIST INCOGNITO

God Is Not

God is not sitting at the scorer's table
keeping track of my progress
He is playing with abandon next to me
He is the coach
He invented the game

God is not the music critic in the audience
He is the violinist playing next to me
The boisterous bass behind me
He is the conductor
He is the music

God is not the CEO summoning me
upstairs for a pep talk or a reprimand
He rolls up His sleeves and works on the line
He is the project and the project manager
He is the motivational leader
He embodies the business
He is the profit

God is not an art collector attending an auction
He is splashing color all over my canvas
He is the subject and the object
He is the art

God is not the editor who proofreads my biography
He is the author and publisher who owns the rights

God is not a vast ocean of indifference
He is the wild current on which I ride

God is not the shrouded mountain peak
He is the mountaineer who holds my hand and guides me
Who carries me when I fade
Who sometimes leaps off the edge of the world
With me hanging on tight

How did I miss it?
He is the passionate lover, not the passive observer
Present and engaged, not distant and detached
The life-giving Lord, not the fault-finding judge

I can't be lost, or lose His love, or His blessing, or my life

Because HE IS MY LIFE

ONE

The Radical Affirmationist

Tell me about the God you don't believe in...
I probably don't believe in him either.

I was starting out on a long cross-country flight, settling in for some uninterrupted study in preparation for a message I would be giving on Sunday. The plane was full so the quarters were close and it took me a few minutes to maneuver myself and my materials into ready-position.

Not wanting to make a scene I slipped my Bible discretely between the pages of a popular gossip magazine on the tray-top and went to work. Finally...lots of time and no distractions. The dreaded airline meal was at least half a continent away.

Jammed into the row shoulder-to-shoulder, it wasn't long before my curious seat-mate interrupted my train of thought. "So, what book is that you're reading?" he asked nonchalantly from a few inches away. Earlier we had exchanged some small talk and my quick take on him was that he was a frequent flier, successful in whatever he was doing, and sophisticated to the point of cynical. "Oh," I said, somewhat defensively and stalling for some exit line to occur to me, "it's, uh, um...I'm reading the Bible." It sounded like a confession.

"The Bible..." Did I detect contempt in his tone, something dismissive? "You must be very religious then." This was his instant conclusion—sounding like an indictment and apparently a bit of a disappointment, as if he had originally pegged me as a peer. As if he had hoped for an intelligent, worldly-wise conversation.

"No, not really" I protested lamely. And I imagined what image he might have of a "religious" person. Other-worldly, ritual-bound, rigid in my thinking, viciously self-righteous. That is my own reaction to the term, truth be told. Now I really wanted to escape this fatally false impression.

So what other options do I have? Do I identify myself by the name of my denomination? What meaning would that have? No, I don't think so. How about "fundamentalist?" I do believe in the fundamentals of the Christian faith. No, the term is beyond redemption. How about "conservative?" Conservative in what way? No, too politically charged. "Evangelical?" My handle in theological discussion. Too aggressive, I decided. Sounds like "evangelistic." Someone who delivers a diatribe against sinners and consigns them to hell. And delights to do it.

Well then, "Christian." Of course. But maybe not. Associations with right-wing zealotry could enter his mind as they often do in depictions by the popular media. Does he think of Christians as narrow-minded, dogmatic and judgmental?

I stared at my Bible in desperation for several suspenseful seconds and focused on the words of the passage that was my text for this coming weekend. These lines from the first chapter of Second Corinthians suddenly seemed relevant to this casual interrogation.

As surely as God is faithful, our message to you is not "Yes" and "No." For the Son of God, Jesus Christ, who was preached among you by me and Silas and Timothy, was not "Yes" and "No," but in him it has always been "Yes." For no matter how many promises God has made, they are "Yes" in Christ. And so through him the "Amen" is spoken by us to the glory of God.

"Actually..." I said out loud, searching for the right words, "I call myself a radical affirmationist."

"A what?!" he guffawed, a look somewhere between shock and amusement covering his entire face, his body shifting toward me as much as the cramped alignment would allow. "Never heard of it."

"Neither have I," I wanted to say, "I just now made it up." But decided not to. Let's keep this conversation going!

"What do they believe?" he demanded. There is no *they*, I thought, there's only me. So here goes.

"I believe that at the center of the universe there is a resounding YES." I stopped for a moment to let this statement sink into both of us. "I believe in the God who says YES. I believe in the God..." and maybe I should have stopped while I was ahead..."I believe in the God who always says YES."

"Always says yes?" he stammered skeptically. "Always? How can you say 'always'? What about the Ten Commandments? 'Thou shalt not, thou shalt not'?!"

Had I gone too far? Was I responsibly representing God's Word in this extemporaneous outburst? How far does the apostle go in his proclamation?

"I believe that God always says YES..." I'm building up steam now, there is no stopping the momentum, "except when he says 'no'..." Did I just shift into reverse? His bewilderment was moving toward smugness when I finished the sentence. "But he only says 'no' on the way to YES!"

We were both hooked. We both needed to figure out what I was talking about, what the Apostle Paul was professing, what God is up to in this world. Beyond religion, beyond politics, beyond the carefully polished stereotypes outside and inside the church that prevent us from believing and experiencing the wild claims of the radical affirmationist. And for the next forty-five minutes we did just that. A preacher and a skeptic in accidental pursuit of an essential, extreme, elusive truth.

Let's get real. What does it mean that God always says Yes? Yes to what, exactly?

Yes to all the promises God has made, according to the apostle's emphatic statement. And his promises—this is so amazing—correspond to our deepest needs, precisely answering our most pressing questions. Not only of Christians, or of religious people, but of every single person who is created in the image of God. Which is every person. Including the man enticed into a conversation he never intended to start. The human quest is universal and so is the invitation to embrace and revel in God's unexpected, unexceptionable Yes.

Am I loved? Every celebrity and every recluse needs to know. Yes! "I have loved you with an everlasting love; I have drawn you with loving-kindness." (Jeremiah 31:3)

Does my life have a purpose? The famous and the forgotten need to know. Yes! "We know that in all things God works for the good of those who love him, who have been called according to his purpose." (Romans 8:28)

Can I be forgiven? The respectable and the reprobate need to know. Yes! In excruciating pain Jesus prayed from the cross for his tormentors—the well-meaning and the mean-spirited, "Father, forgive them, for they do not know what they are doing." (Luke 23:34)

Is it wrong to long for intimacy? Those married and single, happily or not, need to know. No! (which, in this case, is another Yes!) God sympathized with Adam's isolation in the Garden. "It is not good for the man to be alone. I will make a mate suitable for him." (Genesis 2:18) Companionship is God's plan for everyone.

Is there a reliable hope when the odds are overwhelmingly against? The optimistic and the melancholic need to know. Yes! "My hope comes from God. He alone is my rock and my salvation; He is my fortress, I will not be shaken." (Psalm 62:5,6)

Can I find joy in the middle of the mess? The extroverted and the reserved need to know. Yes! "The joy of the Lord is your strength." (Nehemiah 8:10)

What about my physical needs? "Do not worry about your life—what you will eat or drink; or about your body, what you will wear...your heavenly Father knows that you need these things." (Matthew 6:25-34)

What about my future? "Now the dwelling place of God is with humankind, and he will live with them. They will be his people and God himself will be their God. He will wipe every tear from their eyes. There will be no more death or mourning or pain, for the old order has passed away." (Revelation 21:3,4)

Can I get direction for my everyday life? Yes! "If anyone lacks wisdom, she should ask of God, who gives generously to all without finding fault, and it will be given." (James 1:5)

This is only a quick, superficial sampling of the hundreds of promises percolating in Scripture. How they have been suppressed, obscured, forgotten, limited and explained away...is the greatest tragedy. That the church would keep them under wraps, under-appreciated and un-expressed, is bizarre.

The impression that the privilege is for members-only provokes God like nothing else. The divine YES must be shouted not hushed, openly shared not hoarded, directly and specifically applied not simply acknowledged, actively lived not merely enshrined.

All of God's promises are Yes!—are confirmed, are fulfilled, are actualized—in Jesus Christ. He is God's delivery system. When God sends his Son on this personal mission to a planet running on entropy, he is broadcasting a clear signal that must not be missed, to a world that is oblivious. To a world that lives under a death sentence, that must deflect constant threats, that endures demoralizing humiliation, that is scorched by unrelenting doubts—God counters with a rousing appeal. Most transparently, and irresistibly, in Christ.

In the face of Jesus, we see God smile. In his voice, we hear God's tender concern. In his arms extending to the weak and the lonely and the outcast and the cynical, we feel God's invitation and protective power. "Come to me, all who are weary and burdened, and I will give you rest." (Matthew 11:28)

But God sometimes says No. We've acknowledged that. Like the person watching his friend walking unwittingly toward the edge of the cliff. Like the Mom working in the kitchen who sees her four year-old daughter wander into the room and reach out her hand toward the hot stove. "No! Don't touch that!" is what we would expect her to say in a firm, loud voice. If she's attentive, competent and caring. Even though it may frustrate, sadden or anger the child.

But the little girl didn't come into the kitchen to hurt herself—even though that is likely, without an intervention. She's there to be with her Mommy and to explore the magic of cooking. Assuming her mother is a loving parent, her last word will not be No; she will not send the little girl away, denying her, shaming her, excluding her from the joy of preparing a delicious meal. She will find a way to invite her into this wondrous place, to learn from her Mom and become a partner in this creative endeavor.

People may be looking for love in all the wrong places (haven't we all, at some time?) but nobody should ever be shamed because they are looking for love. We are wired for that. God cares, God redirects, God invites us to taste and see that He is good, that He is delighted to provide what satisfies.

As we wander in our quest for a soul-satisfying love, reasonable boundaries that serve a life-saving, life-giving purpose are a great advantage for us. Believe it or not. But a protective boundary must yield to a way forward, if the radical affirmationist is right.

We need to be alerted to a hazard ahead, to the uncomfortable realization that we have gone off-course. But an out-of-bounds marker placed by God is not a full-stop...it is an ellipsis. Because, just then, Someone who knows the way and has our best interests at heart offers to escort us on the path that promises freedom, safety, a return to integrity and real fulfillment.

At the end of this intriguing (to both of us) conversation my partner on this quest sat back and reflected. "How come I've never heard this before? When I think about the Christians I know, I don't hear a Yes. I get the opposite. Why is that? I would have to check out a church that looked like this, if there is one, and I'm practically an atheist."

Overview

Every episode will conclude with a challenge and suggested experiments. Like it or not. I hope you love it! I hope it's the highlight of diving into this book. The best education is Lecture & Lab, input and process, linking head and heart with action. The intentionality, focus and discipline involved will serve to imprint the purpose of our engagement with these themes.

If readers would like to engage the content of this book as a group, I would suggest a simple format based on these generic discussion questions, moving episode by episode...and yet hope that discussion does not substitute for real-life application:

1. **What stands out as you are reading, and why?**
2. **What is still unclear or requires further exploration?**
3. **What is debatable or controversial, and how can we move toward resolution?**
4. **What would you add from your own experience?**
5. **How does this section offer insight into the phenomenon of Christ Incognito?**

The Challenge

Here we go. Would you be willing to wager everything on the Yes that is at the center of the universe—for one week? That even the necessary No can be seen as a wise and welcome detour on the Way to Yes?

The Experiment

1. Read John 4:1-42 (Jesus and the woman at the well in Samaria); Luke 19: 1-10 (Jesus and Zaccheus); John 8:1-11 (Jesus and the woman caught in adultery); Acts 10 (Peter and Cornelius)
2. Say Yes as often as you can...and follow through (this may be dramatically different for you!)
3. When you must say No, find a way to Yes—to fulfill the real need, the deeper desire (this is harder than it sounds, and much better than the demoralizing dead-end of No)
4. Journal and reflect on your experiences during this week
5. Write your conclusion about the claims of the radical affirmationist at the end of the week
6. Revise your view of God, if necessary. Respond and live accordingly...

Amazing Grace

The Truth About Grace

Truth be told, I'm exposed as a fraud
I'm ashamed to face God, I'm fatally flawed
I must hide or pretend or confess

Grace received, I'm starting all over
Not running for cover, not posed as another
Love envelopes me in my distress

Truth and Grace, these virtues together
In full embrace, proud allies forever
One is enlightening, the other amazes
Their merger a blessing, their fusion soon blazes

I'm a huge U2 fan. Snagged tickets to their concert in Vancouver BC and went there with a buddy on a road trip. It was like a worship service. I was warned about that. The atmosphere was festive but also richly contemplative...after Fergie and the Black Eyed Peas finished their frenzied set. It was moving, quietly exhilarating.

When Bono sang a resonant a cappella version of Amazing Grace, the young woman sitting next to me leaned over and asked if he had written that song. She was a Brit born in India. And she didn't know. So, I told her the back story as fast as I could before the thunder and chimes began again. This epic hymn was written to commemorate the conversion of a slave-trading sea captain's ice-cold heart, and as a precursor to the end of the slave trade and the elimination of slavery in England and elsewhere. That's amazing, she said.

If you fear you've written too many checks
On God's kindness account
Drag regrets around like a broken bumper
Huff and puff more than delight and rest
And most of all, if you wonder whether God
Can do something with the mess of your life
Then grace is what you need

[Max Lucado]

TWO

The Wrath of God

The *wrath* of God? Yeah. No thanks.

We'll take the love of God instead, someone says, without quite knowing what it is. Mistaking the superficiality and impotence of sentimentality for the substance of a transforming love.

Consider this. Someone who never gets angry doesn't care. If you are incapable of anger you are emotionally disabled. The opposite of love is indifference, or fear—not anger.

Anger, righteous anger, is love-being-authentic-love reacting against injustice, love responding with justifiable indignation to the powerful mistreating the vulnerable, to any form of cruelty, and to all systems based on a demeaning and diminishing inequality. Love believes in justice because this love cares deeply about people, because love certifies their worth and confirms unalienable rights granted by their Creator.

Love does not remain neutral. It will not tolerate the violation of human dignity. It cannot stand down while damage is done to men and women and children made in the image of God against the command of God.

Thus, love demands justice, requires that protections be put in place, expects fairness, insists on accountability, presides over due process, the prosecution of crimes and the imposition of suitable penalties. You would not want to live in a world where love turns a blind eye toward aggression and oppression, corruption and exploitation, unwarranted deprivation and unlawful seizure, bullying with impunity and rebelling against all standards of decency.

Of course, we do live in such a world...and cry out for some sort of intervention and relief...for someone to love enough to do justice! Unless that day of reckoning happens to come down on us.

Our dilemma is exquisite. We want justice without judgment. We want a benevolent deity without the authority to monitor the edges and enforce the law. We want life on our terms...the same arrangement claimed by those who do their worst.

Love Himself has a better idea.

Enact justice without compromise. Speak the truth, expose evil, validate the verdict. Then, love-to-the-extreme dares to apply mercy by serving the sentence earned by the offender.

Orchestrate the embrace of justice and peace. Match a rigorous indictment against grievous wrongdoing with the impulse toward reconciliation. Call out the crime and insist on repentance—a turnaround, a makeover—and facilitate it. Unleash the power of forgiveness and restoration where none is expected, where hope has been destroyed.

Marvel as wild, unrestrained love and rule-following faithfulness unite—as incompatible rivals, righteousness and peace, kiss. In the interminable debate between Law-and-Order and Liberty-and-Openness we must not miss the paradoxical punch here. The God of Abraham, Isaac and Jacob, as it turns out, is an improvisational genius.

You set aside all your wrath
And turned aside from your fierce anger
Restore us again, God our Savior
And put away your displeasure toward us

Will you be angry forever?
Will you prolong your anger through all generations?
Will you not revive us again
That your people may rejoice in you?

Show us your unfailing love, Lord
And grant us your salvation

I will listen to what God the Lord says
He promises peace to his people, his faithful servants
Love and faithfulness meet together
Righteousness and peace kiss each other
[Psalm 85]

The Challenge

How do we simultaneously honor the demands of justice and the call of mercy? We easily get confused and become paralyzed. Or we lean entirely to one side or the other. Discovering when we do, that justice without mercy is harsh, inhuman, unrelenting, devoid of understanding and sympathy, and ultimately unjust. If we practice "an eye for an eye" the whole world ends up blind. We also realize that mercy without justice is soft, thin, mindlessly permissive, impractical and self-destructive. Moral anarchy is the result. So, both justice and mercy are required—all of both, not simply in theory, but in practice.

The Experiment

1. Read Micah 7:1-7 (harangue against corruption); Matthew 23 (Jesus down on hypocrisy); James 2:1-17 (faith without works is dead)
2. Make a list of the injustices in our world right now that concern you most. Allow yourself to feel the sadness, the righteous indignation, the anger. Can you identify with the victims? Is empathy the avenue to doing justice? How do

we unleash empathy? Imagine how God feels about all of this.

3. Which issue/s of justice do you personally feel compelled to engage? What are you doing about it? What can you do? What will you do? With whom?

4. How can you add the essential element of mercy to the mix? Discipline yourself to think redemptively as you contemplate all the parties involved. You're not done until you do.

THREE

The *Davio* Factor

Where are you now
When darkness seems to win?
Where are you now
When the world is crumblin'?

Oh, I hear you say
Look up, child
[Lauren Daigle]

When did you die?

I was there in my coaching role, hoping to help a church in the Seattle area rekindle its fire. There was no apparent crisis—there was simply and sadly a lack of passion, and purpose.

People were not entirely pleased with their pastor—who was not entirely pleased with himself. He was open to new ideas (that's why he invited me to come) but wasn't sure about the direction he should take or the changes he should be making. The relationship of pastor with elders could be generously described as détente.

The church was in a funk. Nothing terrible going on, nothing much exciting happening either. A lot like many established churches in so many places in suburban America. Sometimes it seems like we are just going through the motions, not really expecting much to happen when we gather on Sunday mornings...but remaining mostly pleasant if mainly bored. It's what we do.

The service began, the sanctuary was about half-full, and it was already beginning to drag. I sat close to the front, wanting to remain anonymous, intending to soak up the atmosphere. There wasn't much.

We sang alternating hymns and praise songs, snapped off the liturgy, and settled in for the sermon. It was more like enduring than listening. I really do like this pastor, we've had some honest conversations. But he's not enjoying church right now—and that shows.

Mercifully, the sermon was shorter than I expected, and we were winding down toward some sort of finale. I was thinking about lunch.

In this church they take the offering at the end of the service, and the music director got up to direct this part. He stood on the floor below the platform and began to introduce the special music that would be presented while the offering was taken. And that shouldn't take long. I was wrong.

The music director looked extraordinarily cheerful I thought, considering we were at the end of the ordeal. Now, I'm being too harsh, it wasn't that bad, it was just terribly dull. It was almost over and we hadn't connected yet—with God, with the people leading us, with each other, with anything that was happening (or not happening).

"For the offertory this morning, I've asked a new friend that I just met to sing a song that he has written." This almost sounds interesting, I thought. I wonder what's coming.

I had noticed him. I knew it must be him. He was sitting in the front row. And I was certain he wasn't a regular. He was way too engaged—even with the sermon. And he couldn't sit still or stand in one place during the music. He bounced. My awareness was mostly subliminal, but I was curious about him...even a little concerned.

The introduction continued. "I was walking out of the grocery store yesterday and passed a man who was selling the homeless newspaper. He asked me for a dollar. I asked him why I should buy his paper and he told me that he would sing a song for me if I did. I said OK...and prepared for the worst." The music director paused for a moment and some of us quietly chuckled.

"He began to sing...and it was beautiful. So I invited him to come to church today and sing his song. His name is Davio. Please welcome him." Polite applause followed.

I was right. The man I had been watching slowly got up and turned around, revealing an enormous smile. A sight seldom seen in this church.

There was something about him. Something out of place, to be sure, but something almost irresistible, right away. There was something about his countenance, his lack of inhibition. Clearly he didn't know where he was and he didn't know the rules.

"Before I sing, I want to tell you my story," he began. Standing tall and reed thin, maybe 60 years old, exuding a distinctive dignity combined with an intriguing (and somewhat alarming) earthiness, his unexpected presence compelled rows of hibernating parishioners to lean slightly forward.

"A couple of years ago, my life was really sweet. I was married to a wonderful woman, had a great job, owned a comfortable home, had my health, had it made.

But my wife died suddenly. I lost the love of my life.

Then I was at work one day and got a call from a neighbor telling me that my house was burning. By the time I got home, there was almost nothing left. I moved in with a friend temporarily until I could rebuild.

The next month I had a heart attack and couldn't go to work for awhile.

Soon after I got a call from my boss who told me that they couldn't hold my job unless I could set a date to return. At that point, I couldn't. He said he was very sorry.

Finally, my friend told me that he could no longer accommodate me in his home. I had nowhere to go and no job to support me. Even if I got well, I was going to become homeless."

We were all riveted by now. We forgot the lateness of the hour, we forgot where we were, we couldn't believe what we were hearing, we couldn't imagine that this man was in our church—taking over church. This was way too much reality for church. But it got worse—which means it got better.

"I didn't know what to do," he said. "So, one day I got up and walked down to the liquor store and bought a fifth of vodka. I took the bottle with me and hiked up to the railroad tracks on a berm out back of a strip mall. I sat down on the rail and drank the whole bottle. Before long I laid down right there and waited to die. What a blessing. A train would come and I was too drunk to move, even if I wanted to."

We were all mesmerized by his words. By the depth of his pain. By the fact that he was here in church telling us all this.

"I should be dead," he said. He paused, recalled the agony, and sighed deeply. "But I heard a voice. It was the voice of a little girl crying out. The voice said 'Mister, mister, please help me. I'm lost. Please help me!'"

"I said 'Go away, I can't help you.' And waved my hand. I didn't even open my eyes to look around. I felt sick. I was so tired. Too tired to move."

"But she kept calling out to me. I didn't answer her again but somehow she found me, took my hand, lifted me up on my feet, I don't know how, and walked me down to the parking lot behind another store. The sun was blinding me and I had to stop. She stood next to me, this little girl, couldn't have been more than 7 years old, still holding my hand."

"Then her mother came out of the store, shouting for her daughter. 'I'm over here Mommy! I got lost and this nice man found me.'"

"Her mother thanked me and walked off with her daughter, leaving me alone and confused, with a splitting headache. All I could do was thank God for sending me an angel and saving my life that day.

And so I wrote this song in my head as I walked home. I'd like to sing it for you now."

He began. And something happened to every one of us in that room. Because something was happening to him. As he sang in a soul-stirring tenor range about the day he came back to life, a torrent of tears poured down his cheeks. He made no effort to suppress the flow. It was incredibly moving, and all of us were melting. The impromptu a cappella performance was impressive, but the spirit of the man was totally disarming. We were all spellbound and defenseless against this spectacle of salvation.

When he finished, the unnerved congregation sat in stunned silence, except for the sound of muffled sobbing.

"I hoped you liked it," he said. "I've written some more songs and I want to record them. If I make any money it will go to help the homeless. I'm doing well now but so many are not. That's why I stand outside the grocery store every Saturday and sell the paper. God is taking real good care of me but so many are suffering..."

The pastor came down the steps and interrupted Davio in mid-sentence. He put his arm around our unexpected guest, embracing him with a grimace, and politely thanked him for his music. It was obvious the pastor was trying to close the service since we were running late. Who knew how much more testimony we might get...and how much more we needed to hear.

But the man who had invaded our sanctuary with his story and his song did not object. He put his arm around the pastor's waist in return and rested his head softly on his shoulder, and spoke no more.

This rarely happens, but at that moment I started to tremble. It was a moment suspended in time. A glimpse of heaven on earth. It felt like church as I once imagined it...the church I still long for.

Afterwards I sat down over lunch with the pastor who was perplexed by what we had just witnessed at the end of the service and uncertain as to what it meant. "From now on," I said, "we're going to refer to this as the Davio Factor." I waited for a response but got none, so I continued.

"That was a blast of authenticity...so rare, so disruptive, so necessary." I'm searching for words, trying to penetrate the indifference I seem to be getting. "This was an outburst of pure passion, an expression of the Gospel of Jesus that hit everyone in that room right in the heart. And we'll never be the same."

"So, do we bring him back?" the pastor wondered out loud.

"Of course, you do! But what I hope you don't miss is where he brought us this morning. It wasn't church as usual—and never should be again! Even though his story is unique, his awakening to God's grace is an invitation to all of us to share our stories without censoring or shame—that will draw us to the mercy that meets us in places of great need, and even greater miracles."

He looked at me like..."What are you talking about?!" Like..."How would we plan a worship service around that?!"

We continued in our conversation for a long time. Because it takes a long time and a new paradigm to debrief a heavy dose of God's Presence. It is mysterious yet obvious. And cannot be programmed, but only anticipated and received and embraced. When love breaks through, you don't want to miss it.

This volley of love brings us back to life, wakes us up, defies our low expectations and overwhelms our well-practiced defenses. Upending our pride and restoring our identity as beloved sons and daughters. How do we prepare for it, discern its overtures and effects, stop neglecting and deflecting and blocking it?

Davio knows. And so do you and I when we dare to take God at his word and let this love have its wonderful, powerful, unsettling way in our anxious lives, in our sadness, in our tragedies, in our complacencies, in the uncertainties of our everyday world.

Are you ready for church?!

The Challenge

The church founded by Jesus is the sacred gathering of God's people to celebrate God's goodness...and the strategic scattering of God's people to serve the world, to demonstrate God's restoring presence and peacemaking power. Our gatherings should be vibrant, alive, a loving embrace, filled with authenticity, even ecstasy, a platform for praise and a model of the community captivated by Christ and concerned for each other.

The Experiment

1. Go to a worship gathering...at any church (your church, if you have one)...and *Be Davio* (i.e., someone who must express their faith and feeling, someone who is so overwhelmed by the goodness of God, the kindness of Christ, that they can't be still)...OR

2. Go to the gathering and *Look For Davio* (i.e., someone who seems to be alive, engaged and responding) and invite him/her into a follow up conversation over coffee to find out what moves them.

3. Summarize your experience (of #1 or #2) in writing...and add to your reflection why the world needs this expression, this spirit.

4. What are you missing? What part of you died? How would your life change if you came alive, if you were born again, if you were fully awake to the presence and promises of God?

CHRIST INCOGNITO

Nature vs. Grace

In this corner: Nature—what is
In this corner: Grace—what comes
It will be a battle, a tug of war
Your soul at stake

Nature—what is
It is what it is, that's all
It is the way things are
It is the way things must be, always will be
And so we do what comes naturally
Because that's what we know how to do
Do what seems right, what feels good,
what works for you
Act according to your nature,
according to the script handed to you
It's all by chance, you don't have a choice
You are hard-wired by instincts and appetites
It is futile to fight them
Obey your urges, give in to your fears
Let it happen, it's your destiny, it's your nature
And if you're lucky, you'll survive,
you'll live another day
Or not, no matter
We all die someday, and that's the end
So sad, to be sure, oh well

Have you heard about Grace?
Some say it's a myth, a fable, a far-fetched fairy tale
Too good to be true, a contradiction, an outrage
It's just not natural
Grace—what comes
Goodness undeserved, love unexpected
Life beyond the limits imposed by nature
A great gift dropped into our lockstep world
Overriding nature
countermanding the compulsion of nature
Overturning the judgment of nature
disabling our fear of death
Grace because of God and his Jesus-intervention
An invitation to life, a life that is super-abundant
To live again, to love with courage
To live as a living sacrifice for the sake of
multiplying grace

In this corner: Nature—what is
In this corner: Grace—what comes
superseding nature
Grace—the One who has come, who is with us now
and is coming again
[inspired by Terrance Malik's epic film The Tree of Life]

Found

It is the hardest thing to admit that we have sometimes lost our way. Our pride won't let us. We prefer to focus on harm done to us. We have much to say about that. But honesty and integrity demand that we face ourselves, that we confront our weaknesses, that we acknowledge our faults, recognizing our own contribution to the conundrum. And then, as Someone reminds us, "the truth will set you free."

Jesus gained the power to love harlots, bullies and ruffians... he was able to do this because he saw through the filth and crust of degeneration, because his eye caught the divine original which is hidden in every way, in every man. Jesus did not identify the person with his sin, but rather saw in his sin something alien, something that did not belong to him, something that merely chained and mastered him, and from which he would free him and bring him back to his real self.
[Helmut Thielicke]

Finding My Way

Finding my way, the best that I could
Trying my hardest, and calling it good
Sometimes obeying the laws of the land
At other times following some other plan

Going with the crowd when the pressure was great
Then off on my own as I carried my weight
Confused when I came to the end of the road
And knew I'd been lifting a heavier load

That's when you suddenly caught my attention
My life, you informed me, was not my invention
Then who is it for and what does it matter
I give you permission all illusions to shatter

Awaiting an answer I stepped out of my pride
Stood still and was thankful for the end of my slide
From somewhere your kindness broke into my heart
And led me, reassured me, I'm ready to start

God help me to do what you want me to do
The only way this is working is trusting in you
Be my friend, my companion, my wilderness guide
Wars raging around me, inside me, about to engulf me
Christ stay by my side

FOUR

The LOGIC of God's Love

The literal translation of *logos* from the Greek is "word," which is entirely inadequate for understanding the depth and force of this concept. *Logos* is not merely the word for "word," but carries the connotation of meaning, of explanation, of premise, of the starting point for discovering the truth—the reality—about something. The logic behind it and within it.

We call the study of living things biology, the study of animals zoology, the study of cells histology, the study of cognition and emotion psychology. The L-O-G-Y at the end of the word indicates our intention to master the subject, to capture and comprehend its essential nature, structure and action. The *logos* of anything is the interpretive key, the organizing principle that opens the door to knowledge.

The Gospel of John starts with an introduction to the Logos—who was "in the beginning," who was "with God," who actually "was God," and "by whom all things were created." John is co-opting Greek philosophy and proposing that a person, this Jesus of Nazareth, was the embodiment of the *Logos*, the key to knowing the God who is by definition transcendent, remote, high and holy, above and beyond us, awesome and at the same time unknowable ("ineffable" is the technical term). John's claim to locate the *Logos* in history among humans is audacious, to say the least.

For classic Greek Philosophy, as first proposed by Heraclitus in 500 BC, the Logos is some version of Reason. Man can reason his way by objective thought and quantitative calculations to ultimate understanding, and with enough effort and data to a grandiose Theory of Everything. But critics have pointed out that Reason is subject to the distortions of emotions and motivations, which are much of the time hidden and unacknowledged. And so, our Reason is more like Speculation, based on hunches, wishes, peer pressure and built-in biases.

For ancient Oriental Mysticism, the way forward is much more exotic and intuitive. Follow your Imagination—the capacity for manipulating the elements, for realigning and even redefining what appears to the senses. Mysticism is extremely, unapologetically subjective, a quest for power that tends toward Magic, the conjuring of alternative realities by a variety of creative and occult practices.

There have been many brave and clever attempts to combine the best (or at least the most attractive, or most marketable) of Eastern and Western approaches into a consolidated, if somewhat unwieldy, even chaotic, world view. The New Age phenomenon is a potent and popular example. Can some expression of this postmodern project succeed? Can the inherent contradictions be resolved, or bypassed, or represented as a sign of paradoxical profundity?

John's Gospel has another background. "In the beginning God created the heavens and the earth," the prologue of the Bible from the Book of Genesis, reveals that God spoke the universe into existence. He simply spoke a Word: "Let-there-be..." and all that is came to be and, under God's sovereignty, to become.

In the Book of the Exodus of the Hebrews out of Egypt, God spoke a Word: "Let-my-people-go..." and then compelled the stubborn, arrogant slave-master to release them. God's Word, inaugurating the national status of Israel, was codified into Law, with the Ten Commands given at Sinai as preface. God's Word was God's covenant with God's people, giving them an identity and imposing God's design for all of their relationships—now to be viewed as sacred, no longer as simply transactional, or as utilitarian, or fated by caste.

In the Old Testament Book of Proverbs, Wisdom impersonates the Logos. The Word becomes intensely practical and specific in the nitty gritty of everyday life. God speaks into the nooks and crannies of personal experience, where we tend to get distracted or confused or lazy or inordinately self-centered, and calls us to the uncommon sense of righteous strategies.

The Prophets of Israel and Judah recapitulate the Law, reminding God's people of the Truth we may abandon, deny or completely forget. The Prophets speak directly, clearly, fearlessly and with the authority of the Logos. They warn of severe consequences—and yet hold out a stirring hope for those who attend to the Word.

Classical Greek Philosophy, and its offspring the Enlightenment, in a noble quest for Reality (what is objectively, demonstrably real), shares the prize for highest human achievement with the esoteric insights of Eastern Mysticism (what the mind can imagine, what Powers of mind and mythology can be unleashed). It's the best we can do, by ourselves, with our considerable intelligence and talents, in a closed system.

It's not enough. Reason degrades into the vagaries of Speculation; Power descends into the dark labyrinth of Magic. The sages of the East meet the geniuses of the West...and we're still scrambling to get to the heart of the matter, to the deep explanation, to the foundational premise, to the elusive Logos.

But the biblical revelation, by itself, is not adequate either.

In Genesis, the Word is credited with creating all that is—and then this creation is contaminated, corrupted. In Exodus, the Word calls a people into existence (who were enslaved, rendered anonymous, "not a people")—and this reconstituted tribe often fails to obey the Word, and so fails to model and spread the Word.

The Proverbs present an ideal that fills up an entertaining volume—that is largely ignored, even by its primary author, the erratic King Solomon. The Prophets are condemned, silenced and exiled, or worse. Even those who hear their Word cannot live up to it. The Word inspires us, obligates us, and then judges us for our inevitable infidelity, for our inability to grasp its meaning and apply its purpose.

As hopeful humanists, we have launched the search for the Logos and gone off in all directions looking for IT—not certain what we are looking for, wandering everywhere and nowhere, drowning in frustration and falling into despair, except when we are boosting a novel theory that gathers devotees for fifteen minutes, and sometimes longer, which ends invariably in disappointment and cynicism.

As spiritual seekers and students of Scripture, we have heard the Spoken Word and read the Written Word. We are on the right track, but it leads to the edge of a cliff, only increasing our insatiable longing.

The New Testament, after 400 years of agonized waiting at the edge of the promise, introduces us (finally! "in the fulness of time") to the Living Word. To the Word become flesh, to God become man, to the presence of God among us, "God-with-us." In the birth of Jesus the Christ, the people of this privileged but disintegrating planet are treated to a tangible encounter in human history with the God who comes to us up-close-and-in-person.

The Incarnation of God, in Jesus of Nazareth who is the Son of God, is the shocking good news that reorients all of life. Jesus the Logos is the interpretive key, introducing us to God—God's character, God's investment in and affection for all of humankind, and God's mission to restore a broken and bloodied world. Unveiling the luminous Logic of the Kingdom of God.

That God would visit us with the intention of rescuing us, forgiving us, blessing us, strengthening us, straightening our path, reconciling our relationships and securing our future...is beyond belief, and our capacity to discover, much less enact on our own. News that is too good to be true...but it is.

This is a New Creation, a Second Exodus, the embodiment of Wisdom, the gift of a humbled heart and an empowering Spirit, an infusion of grace upon grace after grace, endlessly. He, the LOGOS of God, is the life that defeats the hegemony of death, the light that cannot be extinguished by the darkness. And the darkness can get awfully dark.

My wife and I stood in the sanctuary of the First Baptist Church of Sutherland Springs, Texas, less than a month after the one-man massacre that ended 26 lives—men, women and children—and wounded 20 others. The horror of that fresh memory haunted us as we stood in the center of a room that has been turned into a memorial. Placed where the victims were sitting on that November of 2017 Sunday morning were 26 chairs, each with a first name and a single red rose, except for the pink rose representing the unborn child who died along with the others in that terrible mass murder.

Any conscious, caring human being must be overwhelmed standing there surrounded by the stark evidence of unspeakable evil. The darkness of the sadness was suffocating. I have confronted similar soul-crushing scenes (on a much broader scale) in Rwanda and Cambodia and Haiti and Bosnia, as well as in Mississippi, in the Bronx, on the Rez in Arizona, in Oakland California...and in the aftermath of my own sin-saturated stupidity.

But someone has painted this ravaged room reserved for worship... white. The floor, the ceiling, the walls, the platform, all the chairs in the church were awash in white. A dazzling white. As if the darkness could not permanently blot out the light. As if this chamber of horrors had been turned into the anteroom of heaven.

As if pain and suffering and death and loss could be reversed by the Word of promise, by the intervention of a Savior risen from the dead. That in the daring Logic of the Logos, Love is the miracle that triumphs over all enemies, all haters. That this is the will of God, the plan of the ages, the promise to all those who put their trust in God's eternally valid, radically transforming Word.

The Word/Logos that initiates the universe, and the same Word/Logos that sustains what it made, anticipates the sending of the Son who makes sense of our existence, of this world and our purpose in it. Who becomes the one always reliable reference point guiding us through the maze of options and threats, opportunities and seductions that clutter the landscape. Who welcomes and escorts us into the presence of our Abba, our merciful Father. Who fills us with the courage to do the right thing in the most confusing and challenging of circumstances.

The personal, powerful, Logos of God is explicitly profiled in the prologue to John's Gospel. Using the language of classical Greek philosophy, the author who is a follower, places the life of Christ in a down-to-earth context. The heavenly ideal intersects with the down-and-dirty real and becomes good news that is immediate, relevant, accessible and embraceable.

In the beginning was the Word
And the Word was with God
And the Word was God
Through him all things were made
Without him nothing was made that has been made

In him was life
And that life was the light of all mankind
The light shines in the darkness
And the darkness has not overcome it

The true light that gives light to everyone
Was coming into the world
And though the world was made through him
The world did not recognize him
He came to his own but his own did not receive him
Yet to all who did receive him
To those who believed in his name
He gave the right to become children of God

The Word became flesh and made his dwelling among us
We have seen his glory, the glory of the one and only Son
Who came from the Father, full of grace and truth
Out of his fullness we have all received grace
In place of grace already given

No one has ever seen God
But the one and only Son
Who is himself God
And is in closest relationship with the Father
Has made him known
[John 1]

For God loved the world so much
That he gave his one and only Son
That whoever believes in him
Should not be lost but have eternal life
God did not send his Son into the world to condemn the world
But to save the world through him
[John 3]

Jesus, the living Logos, *is "the image of the invisible God, the firstborn over all creation. For in him all things were created...all things have been created through him and for him. He is before all things, and in him all things hold together."* [Colossians 1]

"In these last days, God has spoken to us by his Son, whom he appointed heir of all things, and through whom he also made the universe. The Son is the radiance of God's glory and the exact representation of his being, sustaining all things by his powerful word." [Hebrews 1]

In the last Book of the Bible we have this description of Jesus the Son, the living Word of God: *"Worthy is the Lamb who was slain, to receive power and wealth and wisdom and strength and honor and glory and praise!"* [Revelation 5] Which is the same exclusive language used to honor and adore God.

And then, *"Never again will they hunger; never again will they thirst. The sun will not beat down on them, nor any scorching heat. For the Lamb at the center of the throne will be their shepherd; he will lead them to springs of living water. And God will wipe away every tear from their eyes."* [Revelation 7]

Finally, *"Look, I am coming soon! My reward is with me...I am the Alpha and the Omega, the First and the Last, the Beginning and the End. Blessed are*

those who wash their robes, that they may have the right to the tree of life..."
[Revelation 22]

The Logos is God's final Word, his last speech, his best gift. The Incarnation of the Living Word is a tremendous risk, violating every concern and protocol of conventional religion.

God cannot cross paths with man. For man's sake—we cannot stand in the presence of God, we will be undone, exposed as guilty, riddled with shame, consumed by judgment. And for God's sake—God cannot humble himself, become vulnerable, meet us in our mess, serve us, suffer for us, die for us...can God?! The claim is crazy, scandalous, inconceivable. It is not a scenario that a pious person would ever invent or suggest.

This surprise must be the work of God, flowing from an incredible, unreasonable, previously unimagined reservoir of love. God meeting us where we are—not where we should be, not half-way, not with preconditions of our presumed sanctification. Letting us in on a fantastic secret. Commissioning us to incarnate Truth and Grace, the sacred syntax of the Logos.

I was on my way to meet a friend for lunch in Berkeley. I'm a Cal grad so it's always cool when I get to retrace my steps near the campus...a campus in constant uproar when I was a student there in the late 1960s.

As I hurried on my way I sensed that God was going with me, and wanted to borrow my body and my voice, if the need might arise—which it does, much more frequently than I am prepared for his call.

Across the street, in the direction I'm heading, is a man almost completely obscured by a sandwich board that appears to have his depressing circumstances summarized on the sign. I only read the first sentence. And was planning to walk past. Well, not exactly planning, just ignoring him. But the logic of the Kingdom redirected me, as it sometimes does.

So, Christ asked to borrow my voice to greet his friend. What? OK, that's weird, but whatever. "Hey," I said, forcing myself to sound cheerful. He responded with some inarticulate sound and then looked up, maybe a little startled. "How you doin'?" I asked, with a nonchalant tone...not exactly projecting my Lord's heartfelt interest. Not yet.

He set the sign aside, stepped on to the sidewalk and walked toward me. "I'm doing well," he said, covering up his pain. "But it's been kinda rough lately." And here comes more commentary than I was asking for.

"I'm three months sober, but it's getting harder. I'm waiting for the VA to tell me they have an opening. Staying clean on the streets isn't easy."

An awkward silence.

But prompted again, I asked if I could pray for him. Couldn't think of what else to say.

"Yes!" he exclaimed, "that would be great!" And he moved close enough for the hug I was supposed to give him.

Here we were in an extemporaneous embrace. I wondered if it was legal to pray in public in this secular city, but was encouraged by the One in charge of my life to take a chance. So, I prayed.

When I finished, he stepped back and gave me this huge smile. Which led me to offer some pocket change. "Could you use a little help, a little money today?" He had never asked but was obviously delighted by my spontaneous gesture.

I opened my wallet looking for a five or a ten but, to my chagrin found a twenty. I thought about asking for change...but decided to give it all. With the Word whispering in my ear, I really didn't have a choice.

And then, I said, without meaning to, "Let me give you my card. I want to hear from you when the VA takes you in and you're doing well. Call my cell."

Giving my number to a stranger? What if he abuses the privilege?! What if he does...someone said in a still small voice.

I went on my way, somewhat perplexed and massively energized by this exchange. Realizing I'm not alone, that I'm never alone, and that my life (my time, my money, my interest) is not my own. I want my words to approximate God's Word, my tone his compassion, my message in word and deed an affirmation of the value of the person in front of me, of their potential in Christ, of an invitation to reassess current assumptions and discover the real meaning and uplifting purpose of their lives.

Frederick Buechner writes, "Once believers have met God in a stable, they can never be sure where he will appear or to what lengths he will go or to what ludicrous depths of self-humiliation he will descend in his wild pursuit of humankind. If holiness and the awesome power and majesty of God were present in this least auspicious of all events, this birth of a peasant's child, then there is no place or time so lowly and earthbound but that holiness can be present there too."

Aware of this—of Christ incognito—and persuaded by the logic of God's implausibly self-giving way, a new "formula" for living becomes viable, even irresistible and, by the grace of God, operational in our experience. Living according to the Logos of God's Love generates a personal, powerful, universal appeal.

It isn't logical that God would love us. From any cosmic vantage point of view or human perspective. Even a sentimentalist, with any sense of decency, dismisses the idea.

We are too small, too insignificant, too inconsequential. Too much of a mess. It's fantastic on the face of it. It sounds so crudely anthropomorphic to make such an improbable and uncouth suggestion. Bringing the other-worldly, other-dimensional Creator-God down to earth, to the level of a distressed, dysfunctional creature. Let's be honest about the human condition and the extent of material and moral corruption in our world. Entropy is our reality.

God is way up there (in heaven), way out there (enthroned in holiness), if God *is* at all. God is a force, pure mind, eternal spirit. God by any reasonable depiction must remain distant, detached, uninvolved in the affairs of humankind. It is just too much to hope for. Even the Bible says that no one can see God and survive.

How presumptuous that we should expect God to love us. How dare anyone suggest anything like this. As if we were lovable in our current state. It's easier to imagine the wisest and wealthiest person who ever lived taking interest in a microbe—or a cluster of microbial riffraff—than to conceive of the Supreme Being loving a finite, fallen being so far beneath in the ontological order as to be nothing but "dust in the wind." It's absurd.

But if the God living in unspoiled splendor actually did condescend to love us—let's consider it for a moment, for the sake of argument—why would God conceal his love, why would God hide his greatest gift? It's a shock to even consider divine love, and it would be terribly cruel of God—and completely mystifying—to then obscure the very thing that would certainly mean the most to us.

This is the mystery of revelation, the spectacle of God's initiative—as well as the irony of *incognito* as applied to God's omnipresence and our astonishing, blinding obliviousness. We don't determine or define or configure God's role in his universe. God does. We do well to pay attention to the signs of his presence and power and character everywhere. God will show up when God chooses to in whatever way God decides is best.

That God is Love...is not a logical deduction from some prior postulate, or an enlightened intuition, or a liturgical contrivance, but a revelation broadcast by God into our world in a multi-media blast. Culminating in the coming of Christ to us—which is God up-close and personal disclosing God's very nature and inclination to embrace us as we are, as he finds us, on this earth with his transformative love.

God is Love...here is my take on the evidence of God's existence, nature and impact in outline form. The elaboration of each feature is another book.

Creation : The Universe

The Puzzle of Existence: why is there something rather than nothing?

The Big Bang: who pulled the trigger?

The Laws of Physics: the exquisite calibration of the Four Fundamental Forces

The Mystery of Mathematics: the unreasonable effectiveness of math in all scientific endeavors

The Origin of Life: the appearance, design, differentiation and proliferation of life forms

The Wonder of the Cosmos: endless exploration, experimentation, explanation, bewilderment

The Anthropic Principle: the elaborate fine-tuning of this privileged planet for human thriving

"The most incomprehensible thing about the universe is that it is comprehensible" [Einstein]

Humanity : The Uniqueness

The Miracle of Life: its intricacy, flamboyance, diversity, domains, complexity and dynamism

The Design of the Human Body: elegant, functional, durable and fragile

Childhood: conception, birth, bonding, endearment, innocence and potential

Human Consciousness and Identity, Will and Values, Conscience and Convictions

Human Imagination and Vision, Creativity and Ingenuity, Emotion and Freedom

The Human Spirit: passionate, restless, vulnerable, indomitable, resilient

Connectivity : The Priority and the Drama

The Richness of Human Experience: personality, discovery, story, conflict, courage, endurance

The Warmth and Force of Friendship: the centrality, strength and delight of human relationship

Community and Culture: belonging, empathy, care and synergy, organization and creativity

Spirituality : Hard-Wired for Meaning

Esthetics, Ecstasy and Awe: why do we hunger for beauty?

Good and Evil: moral dimensionality, accountability, justice, ethics and consideration of others

The Spiritual Quest: the relentless search for personal significance, purpose and hope

History : The Meta-Narrative (the Arc of History)

The Gift of the Jews: convicting and compelling ethical monotheism

History of Israel: distinction and destiny, indispensability and fallibility, prophets and prophecies

The Literary Power, Timeless Wisdom, Expansive Range and Pervasive Influence of the Bible

The Life, Ministry, Teaching, Miracles, Death and Resurrection of Jesus Christ

The Centrality and Appeal of Jesus Christ across Centuries and Civilizations

Transformation : The Intervention and its Ongoing Effects

Redemption: fatally flawed humanity, amazing grace and radical transformation

Inspired/Inspiring Global Followers/Emerging Leaders, Sinners/Saints and Servants

God's Love Wins: infinite value, greatest longing, kindness unending, selfless sacrifice

All of the above are broad hints—all accessible for rigorous investigation and careful inspection. But truth is not neutral or sterile. It accumulates into a world view.

A World View is a set of assumptions about existence, a comprehensive system of beliefs, a guide for approaching life. It is the Big Picture.

Following are eight major World View options. There may be some overlap but also distinctive elements in each view in terms of epistemology (theory of knowledge...how do we know what we know?), cosmology (the structure of the universe), psychology (human nature and behavior in its complexity), ethics (discerning right from wrong... if there is such a thing) and eschatology (what we can expect from the future).

The question is: which lens is clearest—which explanation is coherent, congruent with reality, actually helpful for everyday living, and ultimately vindicated by the consummation it foretells? Which means that every world view requires faith.

1. Atheism

Reality: We're alone in a chaotic, entropic, pitiless, materialistic universe (incidentally, most of the universe is missing—composed of dark matter and dark energy, so we speculate—as is our reason for being)

Identity: I'm an accident, that's all, and must bravely make my own meaning...if I can

Strategy: Severe Skepticism permitting unhindered individual Autonomy (making the most of this one brief life, avoiding all manner of superstition, managing a chronic bitterness due to a nagging nihilism)

View of Christ: An eccentric quasi-historical figure who was executed as an insurrectionist and later deified

2. Humanism

Reality: Homo sapiens are lucky to live in this age when we dominate on earth, in a vast indifferent cosmos, on an evolutionary timeline that will soon expire for us...next up: Transhumanism—assimilate with next-gen machines (if we don't destroy this planet first)

Identity: I am a rational being with irrational tendencies that must be subdued

Strategy: Follow your heart, be as happy as possible, ride the turbulence, leave a legacy, accept your fate/extinction (the new stoicism)

View of Christ: an inspirational figure who adds to our curated collection of eclectic wisdom

3. Animism

Reality: The world is enchanted, teeming with gods and goddesses, angels and demons, entities under every rock and spirits around every corner

Identity: I am a pawn in a great conflict between all these competing powers

Strategy: Practicing Magic (secret knowledge and spells to outwit, manipulate and appease the dark forces)

View of Christ: A good luck charm, a shaman with special abilities (sometimes practiced in the form of a syncretistic Christo-paganism)

4. Mysticism

Reality: I live an alternative reality in a pantheistic Universe full of infinite possibilities

Identity: I create it! I luxuriate in my solipsistic paradise.

Strategy: Escape to Ecstasy (exploring my own inner world, maximizing my own unlimited powers)

View of Christ: symbolic of someone who has achieved a state of higher consciousness

5. Fanaticism

Reality: My world revolves around _____ (hero, cult figure, boyfriend/girlfriend, desire for wealth, craving for recognition, hobby, game, addiction, possession, ideology, etc)

Identity: My life is an extension of my idol

Strategy: Absolute Obsession—everything in my life is oriented around my all-consuming dependency

View of Christ: a rival, an associate, an ally or subordinate to the
_____ we worship

6. Neo-Paganism (Postmodern 21st Century Version)

Reality: My momentary desires and my accumulating experiences of the world are all that exist, all that matter

Identity: I self-identify (this may be fluid) and self-determine (living as a protest against conventional social constructs) as an inveterate and unapologetic pleasure-seeker

Strategy: Obey your thirst, satisfy yourself (avoid hurting others), be tolerant

View of Christ: Who? Oh him...a figment, probably an impediment, owned by abusive churches

7. Monotheistic Religion

Reality: there is one, true, living God who is all-knowing, all-powerful, sovereign over all creation

Identity: I fall short of God's high expectations and fear I will never be fully accepted

Strategy: Perfect Performance (trying hard to earn the favor of this distant and demanding deity), remain uncritically loyal to ancient traditions, look your best and stay out of trouble

View of Christ: A good man, a great teacher, a revered prophet

8. Biblical Faith (Christ-centered Spirituality)

Reality: There is one, true, living God who is all-knowing, all-powerful, sovereign over all creation, personally invested in the best interests of humankind, overflowing with compassion and kindness

Identity: By God's gracious decision and through faith in His Son, Jesus Christ, I am God's beloved child

Strategy: Total Trust—living by His Word and in submission to His Lordship over every area of my life as I am filled with gratitude, endure suffering, and am driven by the prospect of ever-increasing joy

View of Christ: A controversial First-Century Jewish rabbi, the promised Messiah, the suffering Servant, the centerpiece of the Gospel, the Savior of the world, the Risen One who is now Lord of all and worthy of total devotion, who will return to overturn injustice and establish a Kingdom of everlasting peace

A world view has profound practical implications, of course. And, in the case of biblical faith, constitutes an invitation as well as an orientation. Facts are subject to (mis-)interpretation and we can distort it, spin it, argue with it, ignore it or submit to it. But with biblical faith that "it" is portrayed as a Person. A person we can't manipulate or domesticate. He is his own Person. We have a reliable record of his words and works. And that Person reveals himself to be loving to the core...in a way we must experience to arrive at real knowledge and unforeseen delight.

He is Christ Incognito because he does not override your will with an appearance or a command you cannot resist. He respects your freedom, including the (terrible) freedom to say *No, not interested, not going to recognize you because of the changes that you will make in my life, because I want to be in control.* Or, you can revise the original eyewitness reports of his life and invent your own religion, to your own detriment—with a reconfigured avatar in your pantheon. But you might lose something(!)

Apparently, God hides to the extent of disappearance if we are looking for God in the wrong place, with the wrong motives, in speculation that showcases our pride or with the desire to fabricate a god to our liking. If we are not ready for the reality, if we are not radically open to the truth, if we are not willing to change, God is silent, God is invisible, God is beyond our reach.

If we choose the sovereignty of the self, God leaves us alone. Until the next time. Love is patient, even longsuffering. But the invitation stands, as long as it does. So much is at stake—the love of a lifetime, for a lifetime and beyond, adequate for our every need, and unmatched in all of creation. A Kingdom of indescribable blessing awaits.

Refusal breeds spiritual insensitivity; indifference constructs a fortress defending ourselves against the intrusion of a disruptive spiritual awareness. We tend to lose track of the Word of God as we tune into other frequencies and their fantasies. But the still, small voice with the sweet, intense tone of Christ can penetrate any barrier to faith, any longstanding doubt, any unhealed wound.

On the other hand, our sadness, our rage, our pain, our depression can render us incapable of perceiving or responding to God's presence. The dark night of the soul is an exceedingly lonely place. Through no fault of our own we may arrive in such a desolate state. But the emptiness we experience there may not be the only reality. The honest and stirring accounts in the Bible and the personal testimony of millions should make us hesitate before pronouncing that God is dead, helpless, indifferent or incapable of redeeming the most miserable situation.

Can God relate to the depth of our pain, the discouragement of our plight, the illogic of our predicament...to the infinite distance between us and God? Consider this striking prophecy from the Hebrew Bible, written 500 years before the birth of Jesus.

He had no beauty or majesty to attract us to him
Nothing in his appearance that we should desire him
He was despised and rejected by mankind
A man of suffering and familiar with pain
One from whom people hid their faces
Surely he took up our pain and bore our suffering
Yet we considered him punished by God
Stricken by him and afflicted
But he was pierced for our transgressions
He was crushed for our iniquities
The punishment that brought us peace was upon him
And by his wounds we are healed
He was led like a lamb to the slaughter
And as a sheep before its shearers Is silent
So he did not open his mouth
[Isaiah 53]

God relates to us, suffers for us, releasing us from the fate we deserve! As utterly unlikely as that seems.

Listen to this description from the New Testament that announces the fulfillment of this prophecy in the life of Jesus of Nazareth.

Christ Jesus, who being in very nature God, did not consider equality with God something to be used to his own advantage; rather, he made himself nothing, by taking the very nature of a servant, being made in human likeness, he humbled himself by becoming obedient to death—even death on a cross. Therefore, God exalted him to the highest place...
[Philippians 2]

Watch the complete change in perspective as a new understanding of his life dawns on us.

> **We regard no one from a worldly point of view. Though we once regarded Christ in this way, we do so no longer. Therefore, if anyone is in Christ, the new creation has come. The old has gone! The new is here! God was in Christ reconciling the world to himself and has committed to us the ministry of reconciliation...as though God were making his appeal through us.**
>
> [II Corinthians 5]

God shows up in Christ—unrecognized, unwanted and yet undeterred; pouring out measureless love and extravagant forgiveness; does what no one else could do in laying down his life; and offers to empower us with the capacity to freely choose (I know, that's a perplexing paradox) to align our lives with grace and truth every day. An invitation that stands to this day.

> **We may ignore, but we can nowhere evade the presence of God. The world is crowded with Him. He walks everywhere incognito.**
>
> [C. S. Lewis]

The Challenge

Is it logical to believe in God? To believe in the sacred value of human beings (all human beings)? To believe in love? Can we put the data of reality into a test tube, under a microscope, or into a sophisticated computer program and expect a definitive, comprehensive, intellectually and spiritually satisfying analysis?

Philosophy in the West has mostly given up on the big questions and is compartmentalized, with a major focus on how language is used. Science and Technology are mostly concerned with details of material composition and the mastery of mechanisms—on answering the "what" and the "how" questions—and scrupulously avoiding the (existentially compelling) "why" questions. Though many if not most scientists, technicians and philosophers can't help but speculate (outside of their disciplines) about matters of ultimate reality—that matter most.

How can we test (and live according to) the Logic of God's Love?

The Experiment

1. Pick a world view (one of the eight) that you don't hold, but that interests you, and describe how love operates based on the logic of that perspective. Put it into a concise paragraph.

2. Based on your own world view, how does love operate? Compose a five-minute speech and deliver it to a friend (a captive audience). Ask for their feedback.

3. With Christ as your model and source (if you are ready to embrace and embody his love), spend a day (or even an hour out there) inviting him to direct and script you. Take a leap of faith!

4. Reflect on this: What is the core, what is the centerpiece, of your life? What are the various values in the inner circle and what do they circle around? Write a Life Mission Statement of 60 words or less. This mini-manifesto would be the Logos of your life—a higher calling derived from an ultimate authority.

CHRIST INCOGNITO

PART TWO

At the End of Ourselves

It's a Cold and It's a Broken Hallelujah...

The late Leonard Cohen and his haunting tune with the garbled scriptural lyrics invites us to consider the plight of people who are desperate for an encounter with God but averse to the judgment they expect from the church that claims to represent God. So they create their own sacred space and sound. Sometimes authentically, sometimes belligerently, sometimes both.

The most imploring, soul-stirring rendition of this iconic song is delivered by kd lang. She says this about the message: "To me it's the struggle between having human desires and searching for spiritual wisdom." In other words, it's a lament for all us who are frequently, even fatally, conflicted and yet still grasping for transcendence.

K. D. Lang sings Leonard Cohen's *Hallelujah* (Youtube)

This is as close as she can get to leading something like worship...to singing a heartfelt hymn of praise to the unknown and/or unknowable

God...to fulfilling her deepest and irrepressible desire for life-giving intimacy...to experiencing the presence and grace of God in church where she would never be worthy of consideration or welcome to journey or allowed to sing.

This song is an anthem of unrestrained longing (written by an agnostic, sung by a Buddhist) and a call to the church...to embrace anyone and everyone in search of the Lord...as they are, right where we are, uncertain and volatile as we/they may be. As does Jesus Who loves, heals and transforms all he finds.

Maybe there's a God above

Listen to the achingly beautiful repetition of Hallelujah as a wistful invocation...that then veers off when it becomes confused, distracted and barely able to imagine an actual meeting with the One desired above all.

Some claim the original composition by Cohen ended with this verse:

I did my best, it wasn't much
I couldn't feel, so I tried to touch
I've told the truth, I didn't come to fool ya
And even though it all went wrong
I'll stand before the lord of song
With nothing on my tongue but hallelujah

FIVE

Bloodbath

Ending the Neverending Cycle of Revenge

You can only love God
As much as you love the person
You love the least
[Dorothy Day]

Love is a power that enables us before it obligates us
The only way to cope with love as a requirement
Is to experience it first as a gift
When we see Christ's cross as God's entrance into our lives
With a love that forgives all
And increasingly fortifies us to love others
Without demanding a return on our investment
[Lewis Smedes]

I refuse to accept the view that mankind is
so tragically bound
To the starless midnight of racism and war
That the bright daylight of peace and brotherhood can never
become a reality
I believe that unarmed truth and unconditional love will have
the final word
[Martin Luther King]

In the spring of 1995, I was invited to join a team of six, assembled by World Vision, to drive through war-torn Bosnia and assess the effectiveness of the relief efforts of this international Christian humanitarian organization. They had been sending badly-needed supplies of food, clothing and medicine while funding mostly local personnel to administer these essential programs. I was thrilled by the opportunity, and more than a little concerned about the conditions we would encounter as we made our way through territory controlled by a patchwork of competing authorities and armies.

Crossing the border from Croatia into Bosnia we went through our first checkpoint manned by an anonymous militia. It was already apparent that this would be a journey immersed in uncertainty and saturated with threats. We would pass through a number of checkpoints, never sure who was in charge and how we would be received or whether we would be turned back, or detained, or worse. Our jeep was identified by a white flag and the symbol of our well-known NGO. We hoped that these signals would allow us to travel unhindered.

Our first stop inside Bosnia was Medjugorge, famous for several decades as a shrine devoted to a modern appearance of the Virgin Mary.

We attended a weeknight service with an overflow crowd jammed into the cathedral now dedicated to her and heard an evangelical message reminding us that in the Gospel Mary pointed to Jesus and told everyone to "do whatever he tells you."

Then we drove to Mostar, a renowned and once-beautiful city now virtually destroyed by three years of heavy fighting. This was my first time in a fresh war zone and it was a surreal scene of jaw-dropping devastation. Most of the city was in ruins and the city had been largely depopulated.

We headed toward the fabled city of Sarajevo, site of the 1984 Winter Olympics, but it was still under siege, and the highway was closed. We were forced to forego our scheduled visit and take a detour over the mountains to our next destination, Zenica.

An impromptu convoy of cars, trucks, horse-drawn wagons and multiethnic refugees on foot slogged slowly up a winding road covered by snow until we reached a roadblock. A large semi had overturned, was blocking the way, and on fire. Everyone was parked helter-skelter and a ragtag mob of strangers was milling around waiting for someone to clear a path.

On the far side of this ever-expanding parking lot stood a drunken partisan with an automatic weapon firing indiscriminately into the air. I was outside our vehicle and began to move toward a large UN tank standing as a solitary bulwark against the outbreak of anarchy. Standing tall and handsome in his pale blue helmet next to the oversized armor was a member of the peacekeeping force assigned to the troubled region.

"Are you worried about that guy over there?" I asked, hoping this soldier knew some English. He told me he was Canadian. "I've got my eye on him," he responded, somewhat stoically. "When do you stop him?" I asked, hoping there was some plan to intervene. "You have to remember," he said, "we are here as observers." He took a notebook out of his pocket and held it up to prove his point.

"If you want to be safe," he continued, "you need to stand behind me because we are only authorized to take action if someone starts aiming at us." I couldn't tell if he was being serious, but I was relieved when the highway reopened after a short wait and we were on our way again.

Over the mountain and down into a verdant valley untouched by the war, it seemed, we were advised by Bruno, our Bosnian driver, to put on our flak jackets. I had almost forgotten about this provision. But this was the time to take special precautions.

It was a lonely stretch of road and Bruno sped through the countryside like we were trying to outrace some sniper's bullet. Later he confirmed that I had guessed correctly. It was all a bit unnerving. And then we reached a town of about 10,000 just outside of Tuzla. Today, I cannot recall the name of that place but I will never forget our visit there.

The former Yugoslavia was comprised of Serbian Orthodox, Croatian Catholic and Bosnian Muslim communities who, before the breakup of Marshal Tito's communist regime in the early 1990s, coexisted in a somewhat congenial relationship. When that political arrangement enforced by an iron-fisted dictatorship disintegrated after Tito's death, animosities and rivalries boiled over into open conflict. Neighbor turned against neighbor as tribal and religious zealotry savaged whole regions of the divided country.

We stepped into a village that had previously known an unusual amount of good will and tranquility, so we were told. All that changed almost overnight it seemed as instability created mistrust which stirred conflict that inspired violence...that would go unchecked. We met people, the survivors of an area-wide genocide, and listened to their stories of betrayal and brutality. Hearing about so much suffering, and seeing the evidence on pock-marked buildings and a dispirited community, was almost too much to take in.

One day we sat with a number of women who represented a new initiative to restore a semblance of civilization in this torn-apart town— women who as mothers were unwilling to wait for the shooting to stop before acting in defense of their families. Where are the men? I wondered...and was told they were away at war, or wounded, or prisoners somewhere, or were drunk, disappeared or dead.

The women sitting in the room had suffered terribly themselves. Some had been held captive in concentration camps and suffered all manner of mistreatment. These are people who had previously enjoyed a modern standard of living—who were now living in a deprived, almost primitive state of survival and subsistence.

A beautiful young woman sat several seats to my right at the table. She was passionate to protect her children, her neighborhood that was still standing, and rebuild her city. She sounded very brave, as did other women who spoke about their hopes and dreams even as they surveyed the rubble of their lives. Later in our conversation, I looked in her direction again as she was speaking and realized as she turned more toward the group, that the right side of her face was missing. The aftermath of taking a shot to the face...and going untreated for too long.

Finally, after listening for a long time, I broke in somewhat impulsively. "What happened here?!" I asked, almost shouting, shaking my head in disbelief. "You all got along so well just a few years ago even though you come from different backgrounds. What happened?!" It wasn't a very coherent question, but I blurted it out anyway. I faced the Western-trained psychiatrist who sat across from me. I assumed she would have an astute explanation.

She paused for a moment, thought about how she should respond, and hung her head for another suspended moment. Finally, she looked at me and our team from another world and said, simply, "The devil got into us."

Silence.

How to explain the outbreak of such evil? Such hatred and premeditated meanness and unconscionable ugliness. It is a mystery. She couldn't say much more, not even with all of her training and sophisticated understanding of human nature.

As our discussion continued, and became ever more candid, it suddenly occurred to me what I represented sitting in this room engaging with these women. I am a man, and men have done terrible things to these women. I am a Christian, and people claiming to be Christians from Serbia and Croatia have become the enemies of these Bosnian

Muslims. I am an American, and as of the Spring of 1995 the United States had refused to intervene as reports of unspeakable horrors inflicted on men, women and children spread across the world. Only the presence of World Vision, as well as any genuine compassion and actual help we could bring, would make us welcome here and now.

A day later I was invited to meet with the local imam. I looked forward to speaking with him—although as an outsider I had no particular wisdom on this incredibly complex and deeply unsettling situation. He greeted me warmly and I was primed for some respectful interfaith dialogue.

He talked openly about the awful things that had happened...and I listened longer than I wanted to. I could not comprehend what he was describing. I offered as much empathy as I could, with as much sympathy as I could muster added for good measure.

Eventually I asked the question that had been on my mind ever since I had arrived in this open wound called Bosnia. "How will this town and these people be healed. Not only their bodies, but their minds, their souls?"

"Forgiveness," he said, as if the answer was obvious. "We must find forgiveness."

"And what does the Quran have to say about forgiveness?" I was curious because my reading of Islam does not include much of an emphasis on forgiveness. I settled in for a theological inquiry.

"Forgiveness is essential. We have no hope without it. And it is hard."

He spoke emphatically. Then he stopped and searched for the right English words in order to give voice to his convictions.

"There are two theories. The first is that forgiveness only happens after you have drawn the last drop of blood from the last living relative of your enemy. Then, you can forgive." When he finished, he smiled at me, incongruously, and I shuddered.

You mentioned another theory?! Before I could prompt him, he continued.

"But there is another idea. Forgiveness happens when you take the hate out of your heart, and give it to God," he gestured as he spoke. "You just let it go, and then you turn your enemy into a friend and bring him close." I was dumbstruck by one of the simplest and most profound—and unexpected—definitions of forgiveness that I had ever heard.

"Tell me, where is *that* in the Quran?" I asked, trying not to sound shocked.

"Oh, we stole it from you," he said with a very broad smile. "You know about Isa ibn Maryam who is the Prince of Peace." (I do!) "He was a prophet who taught us how to love one another. Sometimes we forget that." He went on, and I didn't want him to stop. I love it when a Muslim Holy Man tries to evangelize me. I'm very receptive.

I asked him if he would allow me to quote him on the subject and he quickly said, "Of course!" And then, "We need to learn how to forgive each other here—otherwise we have no future together."

We ended our time in prayer. Holding hands. When I prayed for him and his leadership, and for this community, I closed "in the name of Jesus, the Prince of Peace, the Messiah of mankind." He affirmed my prayer with his own "Amen!" We embraced and he made me promise never to forget this town and to keep on praying.

Hostilities in Bosnia finally ended later that year. The US and its allies finally decided to intervene in the summer to stop the ongoing ethnic cleansing and the orchestrated massacres of hundreds of thousands of civilians in this forgotten land. Not forgotten by God.

The forgiveness taught and modeled by Jesus is the only remedy in a world at war. Forgiveness purchased by his sacrificial death on the Cross is the only adequate payment for the impossible debt accumulated by humankind.

Forgiveness is the only path to peace. Forgiveness (per Theory 2) is the only way out of our impossible moral dilemma and the only way to reconcile justice with love.

The Gospel once preached to me by a Muslim has the power to restore when all hope is lost. This Good News is for everyone regardless of race or nationality or class or culture or religion or circumstance. The unimaginable mercy of God is a gift that alone has the capacity to revive any victim, repair any relationship, and transform any tragedy. Implying for all of us, I am convinced, that we should never neglect to practice what we have freely received.

Humanity harbors a will to power and, at the same time, is hard-wired for justice. We want things to go our way *and* we want everything to be fair for everyone. Clearly, from an honest recognition of this unresolvable dilemma, from a reading of history, and from our own experience, we are on a collision course. It is unavoidable, always ugly, often violent, and sometimes fatal.

When I assert my will, and have the means to enforce it, I will contradict and override the pure principle of justice. We cannot be equal, you must not be as valuable, your concerns are less important, if my will—if my tribe's agenda—vies for preeminence. We are locked into a deadly zero-sum game. With a stalemate (mutually assured destruction) the best we can hope for.

But it's even worse than that. Much more difficult and complex than that. If justice is honored and self-will is suppressed, the objective, exacting nature of judgment demands the blind application of sanctions against offenders. No exceptions, if we are to be fair and equitable.

Justice requires the imposition of consequences, of punishment, whether by formal constitutional authority and appointed law enforcement, or by the intervention of aroused avengers—vigilantes or insurgents or even whole armies amassed in rebellion against governments regarded as illegitimate or inept, or both.

The dissolution of Yugoslavia as a nation of coexisting communities in the 1990s unleashed chaos, long simmering resentments, and a war of all against all. The results were tragic, barbaric and completely predictable, if our theory of human nature with its fault lines, has any validity.

Sure, let's maintain order and insure security by an assumption of good will with a backup of moral consensus, shaming taboos, credible deterrents, mediating courts, and—when necessary—lethal force. If and when that system breaks down, anarchy in the streets/the law of the jungle/the survival of the fittest reclaim sovereignty. Vengeance with impunity and cruelty, as a stand-in for justice, is unleashed.

In Bosnia and Croatia, in Rwanda, in Northern Ireland, in Colombia and Venezuela, in Lebanon and Libya and Egypt and Syria, in Afghanistan and Pakistan, in Israel and Palestine, in Central America and Mexico, in the American South and in American cities. Where has a cycle of retribution *not* broken out...thinking only about our world in the last century? Scorched earth is everywhere, broken communities scar the landscape, refugees continue to wander, even generations after the conflict subsides, the bloodletting slows to a trickle, the fire finally burns itself out.

Into a similarly troubled world 2000 years ago, besieged by a brutal empire, devastated by intertribal rivalries, and sabotaged by willfulness and perversity everywhere, comes a prophet unlike any other instigating a different kind of revolution. Jesus of Nazareth lived and taught a radical, wonderful, shocking message of love. An active, empathic, relentless love for brothers and sisters and neighbors, for the poor and the outcast and the unworthy, for sinners and strangers and enemies.

This love has the will and the power and the means to forgive. To start again, to renew and restore. To turn those far away, those we fear, those who have harmed us into friends. He called us and showed us how to do the impossible, to break the stranglehold of bitterness and vindictiveness, to be liberated ourselves and extend to our adversaries freedom from the captivity of endemic hatred.

Jesus absorbed the pain, endured the insults, sacrificed his dignity, intercepted our judgment, bore his own grievous wounds, bathed in his own blood for our sake, stepped willingly into the ceaseless crossfire of a global family feud, was bludgeoned and crucified in our place, and accepted the death imposed by our betrayal.

His sacrifice ends hostilities, tears down walls, bridges impassable canyons of hurt, heals and reconciles and reinstalls God's will over and against the worst that mankind can do and has done. Invites us to live as a compelling preview of paradise regained...in a world gone mad. By humbly, gratefully receiving, experiencing and expressing the transformational gift of God's mercy.

This is not a heavenly abstraction—this is the earthly incarnation of God as God into the epicenter of our constant crisis. As witnessed, recorded and retold throughout the centuries in every corner of the world...creating one human family out of an impossible, estranged diversity of tribes, tongues, nations, personalities and backgrounds of abuse and despair.

You can choose to ignore the intervention of God taking place in the unique life, compassionate ministry, profound teaching, redeeming death, death-defeating resurrection and contemporary empowering presence of this Messiah, this Savior, this Prince of Peace. Or, after a sober survey of our situation and the other options, you can decide that trusting God and following Jesus is the only spiritual force that can align you with God and bring all of us together. After we have taken such a hard fall and grown so far apart.

The Challenge

We live in a world that is perpetually at war with itself. Everyone against everyone, at times, is what it feels like. Who can blame the pessimist (who calls himself a realist) who can only imagine the worst—and there is ample evidence to support his negativity—and doubts that any proposal will make any lasting difference. On the other hand, there's an idealism, borne of wishful thinking and bordering on blind naivete, that believes in the essential goodness of mankind (pointing to many noble examples) and in the inevitable utopia that we will somehow create. Such an impulse is admirable, if mistaken.

Is there no other choice? Is there a third way—beyond a contrived triumphalism and a self-sabotaging defeatism? Does Christ Incognito—often unrecognized but present and active, passionate and empowering—illumine another way forward?

The Experiment

1. Read Luke 10:1-37 (Jesus sending the 70 on a mission; parable of the Good Samaritan)

2. Choose one of the contentious divides of our era—race, gender, political party, religion, sexual orientation, or ??—and devise a personal plan to take one meaningful step this week into the breach for the purpose of bringing a preview of peace, love and hope. Find a partner who shares your determination. Team up and do it.

3. Document your experience. What were the difficulties, the roadblocks? What resistance did you meet? What encouraged you? What surprised you? What will you do differently next time? What new capacity must be developed? How will you follow up? Who else will you invite to join you in this ongoing Kingdom venture?

Your Sins

Your sins do not disqualify you
In fact, they qualify you
Because Christ came to save sinners like you
Because perfect people do not need God's grace

When you recognize your need
When you submit to his authority
When his grace claims you

Christ immediately goes to work on you and in you
To change you, transform you
To instill his character and produce the fruit of His Spirit

The sweet fruit of love, joy, peace, patience
Kindness, goodness, faithfulness, gentleness and
The powerful capacity of self-control

Removing what doesn't belong to you anymore
What interferes, discourages and destroys you
Forgiving you, releasing you, empowering you

You are now a miracle in the making
A trophy of God's mercy
Becoming a gift that fascinates the world

SIX

Powerful Parables

The Story that Tells Your Story

The random person next to me on an eight-hour flight from Amsterdam to Washington DC a few years ago was an animated, highly educated and very articulate young woman named Oxana. She was born and raised in Russia but had recently emigrated to DC to start a new job. I was immediately intrigued by her background and we were soon engaged in a conversation about religion. She started it.

"I was raised an atheist," she volunteered in her solemn slavic accent, "but I was introduced to Buddhism a little while ago." She paused, then asked me if I knew anything about Christianity.

"Yes," I said, sensing a set-up of some mysterious sort, but decided to defer. "Tell me what you know about Buddhism," I asked. "Let me tell you a parable I heard," she responded.

It went something like this...

A tiger was chasing a mouse through the forest, almost catching the unfortunate creature several times, but again and again the small rodent escaped the claws of the powerful predator with a series of clever moves. Finally, the mouse ran to the narrowing edge of a high cliff, and this time there would be no possibility of escape. The tiger crouched low and slowly approached its trapped prey. Sensing the end was near, the mouse backed over the edge, legs dangling, hoping against hope that there would somehow be a ledge below that would provide safety.

It was not quite a ledge, but the mouse was able to back out on to a vine, about three feet long, thick enough to hold its weight for a while—its little body now just beyond the reach of the ravenous tiger. The tiger gripped the edge of the cliff with its huge paws, jaws poised for the kill, and waited. The trembling mouse looked up at the menace above and down at certain death below.

End of parable.

"What do you suppose it means?" I decided to ask her, as I indulged in my own speculation. "I don't really know," she offered. "But I suppose this parable tells us that it doesn't really matter what happens to you, or what you try to do about it, there is always more suffering, and no way out, so you realize the futility of it all and just give up. And that makes you enlightened."

She thought for a moment and then said, "Anyway, my friend who told me the story said that the parable teaches us not to hope for too much or try too hard. In fact, since desire causes suffering, if you can suppress all desire you will never be disappointed and you will finally stop suffering."

In the silence that followed, the spare moral of the story began to sink in. Embrace despair. Quench all passion. Care less. Lower expectations to as close to nothing as you can. Achieve complete detachment, the serenity of self-extinction. And then, tiny stranded mouse, you will stop trembling.

"Do you have a parable...a Christian story?" she asked, breaking the tension we were both apparently feeling. "There are a number of parables in the New Testament," I told her, "but there is one that is my favorite."

"Tell me, please!"

Many of us have heard it before. It's quite famous but not always fully appreciated. And, I think it is safe to say, quite different from the story I had just listened to.

It goes something like this...

A man had two sons. The younger of the two sons came to his rich Dad one day and demanded his share of the estate—in advance. The father agreed and the young man left.

My Russian friend interrupted me, with a fair amount of indignation in her voice. "What?! No son would ask for his share of the estate before his father died! That would be like saying to his father—I wish you were dead already! And the father would punish him harshly for his defiance. He would most certainly disinherit him right then and there."

"You're right," I said, suppressing a smile and acknowledging the appropriateness of her protest, "let me continue."

The young man got as far away as he could and bankrolled a rollicking non-stop party. Until he ran out of money, and friends, and a future, much sooner than he had planned. The next day, he had to look for work. All he could find was a job slopping pigs at less than minimum wage, which left him so broke and starved he actually scavenged in the mud for leftover cornhusks.

"Stupid man!" Oxana opined, shaking her head. "Got what he deserved."

But then he came to his senses. He thought about home and the kindness of his father and how he might return and apply for a job there as one of the hired hands. At least he would eat. Even though it would be a long shot, at best, considering how badly he left.

"Oh," she interrupted me again. "If this were a Buddhist parable it would have ended right there. Lay down and die, young man. Your suffering will soon be over. Or come up with a new get-rich scheme!" She laughed out loud at her own suggestion.

I continued, trying to anticipate her reaction to the unexpected un-folding of this improbable parable.

The young man headed back to the place he once called home. Along the way, he rehearsed his overdue apology, hoping it was adequate, that it would sound heart-felt, that he would catch his father in a good mood. He was excited and terrified.

"This is going to be good," my seatmate said, on the edge of her seat, staring at me from close range. "What happened when he got home? Does the story end here as he trembles on the edge? This is not going to turn out well for him." The suspense in our row of two intensified.

It was the end of another long day and the father sat on the porch, as was his habit, gazing out over the horizon. A speck appeared on the road in the distance as a small silhouette beneath a setting sun. The father's eyes followed the slow-motion apparition as it trudged down the path. The object was unfamiliar in both its form and gait.

In a moment, the father recognized him. It was the lost boy bent over. It was his son. Throwing all restraint aside, he hiked up his robe and ran toward the forlorn figure. The young man was taken aback by the spectacle of this great man running and wondered if rage was propelling him toward the one who had earned the full fury of this long-delayed confrontation.

As his father got close, the young man fell to his knees, face to the ground, awaiting his father's outburst. If I can start my apology before he strikes me, he may be willing to hear me out, he thought, and so he began his well-practiced speech.

When the father was right on top of him, he cut him off. What happens next?

At this point, I realized I could not improve on the text itself, so I pulled out the Book and read it. Just happened to have the Book handy.

But while he was still a long way off, his father saw him and was filled with compassion for him...he ran to his son, threw his arms around him and kissed him.

"I'm sorry, I don't believe it," Oxana spoke almost matter-of-factly and put her hands up to stop me from reading any more. "No father would let his son leave home like that and, even if he did, no father would ever welcome him home. It would never happen like that!"

Wait, I said, it gets worse.

The son said to him, "Father, I have sinned against heaven and against you. I am no longer worthy to be called your son."

I saw my new Russian friend nod in agreement with the son's somber and disqualifying assessment.

But the father said to his servants, "Quick! Bring the best robe and put it on him. Put a ring on his finger and sandals on his feet. Bring the fattened calf and kill it. Let's have a feast and celebrate. For this son of mine was dead and is alive again...he was lost and is found." And so they began to celebrate.

I looked up quickly after I read this paragraph—anxious to see the reaction it had provoked. I half-expected her to explode, and it almost looked like she might—her cheeks were blown out and her brow etched with astonishment. But she was speechless.

Eventually she spoke. "I liked the other story about the tiger and the mouse better. Well, it's not better, it's terribly bitter, but it's more believable. Life sucks and then you die. That makes sense to me. This—this story is—this story is *impossible*. There is no father like this father. Nowhere on earth. This story is too good to be true."

And then she looked intently into my eyes, as if she were asking the deepest of all questions and counting on me to be absolutely honest. "Is this supposed to be a *true* story?"

It's a parable. Jesus invented this story. But in it he is presenting a *true* picture of our Heavenly Father and the transforming power of his unexplainable compassion.

It *is* too good to be true, too relentless in its insistence on mercy, even as it resonates with our most anguished and irrepressible longing. It's so hard to believe, it so disrupts our conditioned assumptions...and yet so hard to let go of the fierce appeal of the good news in this narrative.

Far from suppressing our longing, our desire, our passion...from banishing this hope for forgiveness, for acceptance, for unconditional love, for embrace and belonging...it stirs it up, arouses it and elevates it. Even increases our suffering until we find what we were created for and are ready to immerse ourselves in this irresistible gift.

Watching her, I longed for this to be Oxana's experience as she listened, imagined, resisted and, at the same time, felt overwhelmed (I prayed) by a wave of fatherly affection.

We talked longer about many things—some lighter, and then would be drawn back to the topic. This was an eight hour flight!

Later, as we were descending, she turned sideways, took one of my hands and revealed some inner reflections. "I'm still thinking about the two parables. I have lived another story altogether...in between these two extremes. Between your Christian faith in this ridiculously good God and the much more reasonable belief in blind fate and a brave resignation to it."

"I have lived in a twilight zone where we were taught to trust in the state for everything we needed, to excel as our required contribution, and not to worry about big questions that have no relevance to our everyday lives."

She pressed on with the logic of her original world view, now challenged by two powerful parables. "We had no story. We had no need of one. Stories are for children. And besides, individual lives don't really matter."

There was a weariness, an unbearable heaviness in her tone. That might be lifting.

"Thank you for talking to me," she said. "I expected nothing from this flight but to get home safely. Now, I will have to think about these stories, and what my story will be."

Thank *you*, Oxana. Welcome home.

The Challenge

The meaning is in the story. The meaning bleeds through the narrative. Which is why we have to listen with our ears, with our minds and with our hearts. We have to hear what is not spoken aloud but only whispered, what is suggested, what is implied, what cannot yet be acknowledged. There is ambiguity in our stories, paradox, uncertainty and open-ended exploration. There is tone and texture and turmoil that must be distilled. The telling and the interpreting is a matter of sincerity, of skill, of cultural sensitivity and relational connection.

The Bible is the greatest story ever told. It is not an encyclopedia of religious truth. It is not, strictly speaking, a systematic theology. And yet it is a bold statement of truth—in story form, with commentary, and occasional overarching conclusions.

But even the great didactic portions (the Sermon on the Mount, for instance) are filled with misdirection, suspense and provocation. This is heart-to-heart communication in a certain context (with stories behind the stories)—available to all but requiring a commitment to engage with everything in me. The Bible is all the while reading me and teasing the truth about me (the sweet and the sordid) out of me. God is speaking here...calling me, calling you.

The Experiment

1. Re-read the parable of the Prodigal (Luke 15:11-32).
2. If you identify most with the younger brother, write a defense of his decision to leave home. If you identify more with the older brother, write a defense of his reaction to his brother's homecoming.
3. Debunk your defense.
4. What is the good news for you in this parable?
5. Ask a friend (over coffee, take some time) to tell you what story (famous or not) in some way reflects their own experience. Where is Christ in their story?

SEVEN

The End of Religion

There isn't a raging interest these days in organized religion. Been there, done that, many would say. Not sure what it is, don't think I'd be interested, many others would say. At least if we're still young and slightly cynical (who isn't?). Spirituality, on the other hand, is something altogether different from religiosity—though we tend to get them confused.

Religion is about externals. It is the meticulous practice of customs, the diligent enforcement of codes, and the careful replication of ceremonies that are defined and required by sacred tradition. It is a prescribed performance, a pious posturing. It engenders a competitive perfectionism, a put-on purity, an elaborated protocol.

Religion is the incredibly presumptuous attempt to organize and standardize spirituality. It is a two-dimensional, hopelessly provincial, mass-marketed pseudo-spirituality. It is outward, contrived, conformist, coercive, ritualistic, anachronistic and terribly self-aggrandizing—even while professing a humble faith.

Some people would call this *bad* religion . . . in an effort to rescue the form from its many corrupting influences. But the form itself—the ambition to manage God and script our response to God—is the great impediment, the biggest stumbling block.

Religion—any and every kind of religion—needs to recruit us, strip us of our diverse and colorful personalities, fit us into stiff starchy uniforms, hand us a thick sterile rule book, and reduce all mysteries to staunch stale mantras. It is a rigid system that demands unquestioning compliance, creates sanctimonious elites, and condemns everyone who is weak and sinful and insubordinate. In exchange for your loyalty, it provides nothing you need and burdens you never knew you were entitled to.

Religion claims that it can save your soul, but it has no way of getting to your heart. Religion is, and must be, superficial and statistical. It counts bodies (*membership*), dollars (*stewardship*), and duties done (*churchmanship*)—publishing all the propaganda necessary to underwrite its institutional agenda (*bullship*).

No wonder Jesus reserved his severest criticism for the religious leaders of his day. No wonder they hated him! "*Hypocrites*," he called them. "*Proud enemies of the people! Blind guides! Full of greed and self-indulgence! You are like white-washed tombs*," he said to them, pulling no punches. *"You look beautiful on the outside but on the inside you are full of dead men's bones. You appear to be good, but on the inside you are rotting."*

"On the outside, you appear to be..." That's all religion cares about. That's all that matters. *"But on the inside, you actually are..."* This, then, is the deeper concern of spirituality. To take an honest look beneath the surface, behind the appearance, beyond the words. To assess the spirit, the core of a person, the reality on the inside.

You may not be religious ... especially fond of stained glass windows, organ music, ornate cathedrals, clerical collars or evangelistic sermons ... but we are all spiritual. There is more to us than meets the eye and there is more to our lives than the routines.

Our innate spirituality compels a serious search for meaning. It drives us to discover and recast our character. It is about the recognition and reviewing of our values. It is the capacity to connect with other very spiritual, very human beings. It calls us to choose and to take responsibility for our freedom. It leads us to reflect, to explore, to love, to give, and even to selflessly sacrifice. We are more than machines, more than the sum of our animal instincts, and more than mindless devotees fulfilling our tedious ecclesiastical obligations. Much more.

So ... a daring question for us to consider. Now that we've thoroughly thrashed the alternative. Now that we're feeling elated, liberated, and a bit lost. What would a spiritual person look like, act like, be committed to—whatever religious (or irreligious) background this person might come from? If Jesus himself—he who pointedly provoked the wrath of the religious establishment—were selected as *a* (or even as *the supreme*) model of spiritual integrity and energy, what could we learn from him? Could we gain by evaluating other attractive examples of spiritual vitality? Who appeals to you . . . and why?

More and more Americans regard "organized religion" as irrelevant. It seems out of date and out of touch. They can live without it.

But...there remains a hunger for spiritual reality. For many of us it's a ravenous hunger. To connect with God (is that possible?), with other people (how do we find each other?), and with myself (so many contradictions to resolve!). If this is the challenge-of-a-lifetime, what is the spiritual solution? And how exactly does spirituality translate into our everyday human experience?

Three qualities come to mind that would describe someone who is getting it together spiritually. These attributes vividly illustrate the contrast between religion (emphasis on the outside, on the image, on passive resignation) and spirituality (focus on the inside, on the essence, on dynamic involvement).

A spiritual person is, first of all, authentic. He or she is willing to take out their heart, all bloody and beautiful, and put it on the table. This is who I am. This is what I believe. These are my doubts. These are my wounds, my dreams, my fears, my shortcomings. I want you to know me. I will not hold anything back. I will disclose myself to you, I will be transparent and vulnerable with you.

What a huge risk! Do I even know who I am? Do I know what's inside me? Will I get to know myself better as I try to reveal myself to someone else? I have been hurt and disappointed before when I've done this. But if I intend to be authentic, I have to do it again. I'm very tempted to hide my heart, to guard my feelings...but I'm determined to become an open and healthy person.

Secondly, and sequentially, a spiritual person is empathic. Once I have dared to show you my heart, I am now able to invite you to show me your heart. And if you decide to take this same breathtaking risk, I promise I will be gentle with you. I promise to take you seriously. I may not always understand, but I will try very hard to. I may not always agree with you, but I'm still here and I still care.

I assume that you are fragile like me. That you respond to tenderness, to kindness, to someone who suspends all judgment and simply listens. To someone who gives you time and genuine interest. I will engage you even as you have trusted me with the secrets of your heart—and we will have a heart-felt dialogue. I want you to find affirmation, courage and hope in this intimate conversation.

Finally, and crucially, a spiritual person is a connoisseur of grace. Authenticity and empathy require such enormous risk that most of the time most of us retreat from these wonderful, dangerous opportunities.

There's just too much pain. I've tried it and it didn't work. What if I make a fool of myself (again)? What if they don't care? I could stand the anger (maybe) but not the indifference. I'm not ready yet. I'm a private person. Nobody in my family ever did this. I'm a man, after all. I don't know what you're talking about. Couldn't I just pray instead (and avoid being authentic with God, too)?

Grace tells me and you that our risk is covered. That it is worthwhile.

I take out my poor heart. You take out yours. And then, somehow, we encounter the heart of God, the very inside of God. And what do we find there?

We find grace! What a surprise! God is love. Unembarrassed, uninhibited, unrestrained, unrelenting love. Love for us. For each of us as individuals. Grace, it turns out, is at the heart of the universe. Grace sets the pace. Despite appearances, and despite the rantings and threats and dullness of religion, grace gets the first and the last word. We can be authentic (a rare and amazing occurrence in our world) and become empathic (a powerful, irresistible gift) as we let ourselves fall in love with God's heart-full of affection for us.

In fact, we know about this spiritual algorithm by watching God take out his heart, recklessly disclosing himself to us. He holds nothing back. He came into our world and poured himself out. Isn't that what Jesus means, even if formal Christianity—the layers of legalism and liturgy—often distorts this meaning? And God is seeking out a real response, longing for a real relationship to begin and to grow, pledging himself to deliver us from despair as we cautiously, awkwardly invest our very souls in this passionate love affair.

I'm convinced that most of us are eager to live spiritually rich and meaningful lives. We don't want to be captivated by our own shame, by our own fears, or by some solemn and repressive religious system. Our aversion against auditioning for acceptance and appeasing the critics is so strong—and it should be. We can't ever win. After we've jumped through all the hoops, we're exhausted. Though we've memorized all the dogma, we're dissatisfied. When we've swallowed all the rules and regulations, we get indigestion. And, after all that, it seems we're even further away from true spirituality.

That controversial, incendiary document, the Bible, talks about "the spirit" and "being spiritual" all the time.

"*True worship is in spirit and in truth*" (presumably, then, not faked or fabricated) [John 4].

"*The fruit of the Spirit is love, joy, peace...*" (not affectations, artificialities and petty pomp) [Galatians 5].

"*The word of God penetrates* (our defenses and pretenses) *our spirit, sifting the thoughts and attitudes of the heart.*" [Hebrews 4]

"*True religion* (the term "religion" throughout the Bible is only used negatively and critically...or ironically, as it is here) *that God our Father accepts as pure and faultless is this: to look after orphans and widows in their distress and to keep oneself from being compromised...If anyone considers himself religious (a likely scam) and yet does not control his tongue (which misrepresents and demeans and condemns) he deceives himself and his religion is worthless.*" [James 1]

"*I hate, I despise your religious feasts (thunders the prophet who represents God to our conscience). I will not accept your offerings. Away with the noise of your songs. But let justice roll on like a river and integrity like a never-failing stream...Come now, let us reason together. Though your sins are like scarlet they shall be as white as snow, though they are red as crimson they shall be like wool.*" [Amos 5]

Peter, one of the first followers of Christ and a leader in the early church, put it this way as he argued in front of the other apostles and elders for the full inclusion of Gentiles (non-Jews, the outsiders): *"You know that sometime ago God made a choice among you that the Gentiles might hear from my lips the message of the gospel and believe. God, who knows the heart, showed that he accepted them, by giving them the Holy Spirit, just as he did us. He made no distinction between us and them, for he purified their hearts by faith. Now then, why do you try to test God by putting on the necks of the disciples a yoke that neither we nor our fathers have been able to bear? No! We believe it is through the grace of our Lord Jesus that they are saved, just as we are."* [Acts 15]

Let's get to the root of the matter, God challenges us. Let's risk it all. The exclusive religious clubs you compulsively create and fight to control obscure the truth because they don't reach and reshape your heart. Please hear me. Don't withdraw. Get to know me. Taste and see that I am good. I am for you. I've come to you . . . will you allow me to embrace you? I will live in you, forgive you, heal you, comfort you...and you will live with me—now and forever. Trust me. Don't miss this adventure!

How I wish I could announce the end of our isolation, the end of our alienation, the end of religion . . . and the beginning of our new life secure now in God's love. But I don't have to. God already has.

Christians have always tended to transform the Christian revelation into a Christian religion. Christianity is said to be a religion like any other or, conversely, some Christians try to show that it is a better religion than the others. People attempt to take possession of God. Theology claims to explain everything, including the being of God. People try to transform Christianity into a religion because the Christian faith obviously places people in an extremely uncomfortable position—that of freedom guided only by love and all in the context of God's radical demand that we be holy.

[Jacques Ellul]

The Challenge

Christians grow tired of hearing "I'm spiritual but not religious" as an excuse for not being involved in any faith-related activity. But maybe they're right, maybe "religion" is tiresome and tedious and tends to fabricate a fake persona. Maybe the New Testament (the whole Bible, actually) deconstructs all the scaffolding of religiosity in order to call us to reality, to relationship, to the kind of transformation that religion ignores, avoids and even opposes.

The Experiment

1. Describe a time when you witnessed religion failing and what the effect was on you and others. Looking back, what was the real problem? What would a Christ-centered, spiritually rich church look like? Write a proposal for such a community.
2. Ask two friends—one a Christian and another non-Christian—to critique your proposal.
3. Revise your proposal.
4. In what way/s are you still religious? Why?

EIGHT

Life's Secret Sauce

We do not draw people to Christ by loudly discrediting what
they believe, by telling them how wrong they are and how
right we are, but by showing them a light that is so lovely that
they want with all their hearts to know the source of it

[Madeline L'Engle]

I t is the impossible dream. Isn't it?

Joy. The most elusive of all experiences.

Joy. The deep craving of our souls. The longing not easily suppressed.

Joy. Pretending we no longer care, that we no longer believe in such a thing, at least not for ourselves as we survey our joy-deprived lives...we still instinctively search for it, hunger for it, plead for a taste, a glimpse of the real thing.

But what is it?! We are hard-pressed to define it though we might approximate it by sharing an impression from a dream, an unexplainable appetite for ecstasy, a moment of incandescent wonder.

Where in this world do we find joy? We must even if we can't. God help us.

The Quest

So, we read...

There were shepherds living out in the fields nearby, keeping watch over their flocks at night. [Luke 2]

Shepherds. Doing a dirty, thankless job. Working outside, exposed to the elements. Working all hours, including the over-night shift. It was cold, dark, desolate and dangerous back in the day. Endless hours of boredom haunted by the constant awareness of predators prowling the open range and the perimeter of the sheep pen.

Tending sheep...a necessary but dead-end job, hardly an honorable occupation. Nobody respected shepherds. They raised the sheep that were used in the temple sacrifices but they were not allowed to participate in temple worship. They were considered unclean due to their dirty work. Shepherds were not allowed to testify in court because of their unconventional, anti-social way of life out on the margins.

Some irony there, considering what is to come...in a world filled with hard lives, rigid rules, alienating circumstances, embittered attitude and abundant irony.

Then, suddenly, without warning...

An angel of the Lord appeared to them, and the glory of the Lord shone around them, and they were terrified.

In an instant their isolation and the monotony of their meaningless-ness was interrupted by a routine-shattering presence. A dazzling messenger, both intimidating and appealing, broke through their long-practiced apathy, their disguised despair.

But the angel said to them, "I bring you good news of great joy for all the people. Today in the town of David a Savior has been born to you. He is the Messiah, the Lord. And this will be a sign to you: you will find a baby wrapped in cloths and lying in a manger."

Joined by a sky-wide flash mob, driving home the strange invitation.

Suddenly a great company of the heavenly host appeared with the angel, praising God and saying, "Glory to God in the highest heaven and on earth peace to those on whom his favor rests."

That's it. Bombastic brilliance. And they were gone.

If this were Disneyland we would ask when the next show was scheduled to begin. A replay of Phantasma at midnight.

But this was a one-time spectacular and wasn't staged as entertainment. No, the action and attraction was actually elsewhere.

The message was arresting, invigorating, a long lonely time in coming. God shows up tonight. In Bethlehem. Once before, the City of David. Then, a small out-of-the-way village.

In Bethlehem?! As a helpless baby in some back alley lying in an improvised feeding trough? Not what anyone would expect. But spectacularly Good News beyond all expectations.

Good News sending the shepherds on an impulsive, improbable search.

When the angels had left them and gone into heaven, the shepherds said to one another, "Let's go to Bethlehem and see this thing that has happened, which the Lord has told us about."

So they hurried off and found Mary and Joseph, and the baby, who was lying in the manger. When they had seen him, they spread the word concerning what had been told them about this child, and all who heard it were amazed at what the shepherd said to them.

The shepherds returned, glorifying and praising God for all the things they had heard and seen, which were just as they had been told.

The shepherds were roused and energized by the Good News and rushed to the scene of the Messiah's birthplace. When you hear good news, it provokes a reaction. You can't sit still, you can't stay quiet, you can't keep it to yourself. You can't. And if it's really good news, you'll never forget it, you won't go back to life the way it was. How could you?!

According to the angels, and considering the overriding importance and relevance of this Good News "for all the people"...it immediately and continuously incites Great Joy. Or as the text literally describes it: Mega-Joy.

It is an uncontainable joy that pries people loose when they have been stuck, even when they have been paralyzed. "Let's go!" the shepherds shouted to each other. Those who are sedentary and sleepy race toward the promise of a long-awaited and often-in-doubt fulfillment.

"Let's find this, this, this...this thing!" They don't even know what to call it. They've never seen anything like it. It is reported that the townspeople were "amazed" by the testimony of the poor shepherds— that these low-life outcasts would even come into town, that they would talk to people above their pay grade, that they would be so consumed by their experience that they dared to claim they have seen the Messiah, that he's actually here! Could it be?!

The Question

The question must be asked, and explored. What is joy?

A feeling? For sure. A fantastic feeling. But more than that.

Joy is the deep settled conviction that God is for me. It is the consequence of Good News that turns out to be the best possible news...that is definitely too good to be true. Except by some incomprehensible miracle, it is!

That God loves me. Loves us. Loves the world. That God is, as it turns out, an unreasonably, outrageously kind, merciful, relentless lover.

Proving his claim by coming in Person to embrace us with his Love. Comes into our world of pain and poverty to convince us of our worth—in the unimpeachable estimation of our Creator. Calling us to Life—life in super-abundance, compelling us to respond with absolute trust and complete surrender as the trajectory of joy overtakes the entropy of self-aggrandizement and self-loathing, of sin and sadness, of degradation and death.

Joy is the intrusion of heaven on earth. Joy is the invasion of the future into our present tension. Jesus, the baby in the manger, is Immanuel—God with us. God come down to us. God come for us. God investing himself in the human drama with a shockingly redemptive purpose. All to instill an unspeakable joy...that must be shared.

Joy is often relegated to the experience of a far-off heaven. But remember, heaven has broken through. It is eschatological joy—the empowering presence of the future.

Jesus the Christ images the huge heart of God. We now have an up-close and in-person encounter with God in Christ. So, joy is here and now. Joy frames and reinterprets all of our experience, giving us strength we never knew we could have and urgently need.

The joy of the Lord is your strength, Nehemiah tells the ancient Israelites as they gather in their season of suffering to consider their relationship with God and their prospects for the future. If that is true, if joy is meant to be a present reality as well as a distant hope, then joy is not the goal we are working toward, it is the gift we are working from.

Joy changes everything, today. Its impact hits me, transforms me, now. We desperately need a supernatural strength for the problems and challenges we face here and now. What will be later on, according to God's Word, becomes a certainty we can count on, assures us of the value of our efforts—against all odds—and frees us to live and love abandoned to God's cause.

Joy is the serious business of heaven, says CS Lewis, a literary giant from the last century and apologist extraordinaire. It is also our privilege in this moment. Unalloyed joy is *not yet* possible—but God's real presence with us and our high confidence in his reliable character and future provision right now mean we are *already* on this joyful journey to joy. The adventure you must not miss.

Beyond the Brand

By definition, an evangelical is someone who believes and embraces the "evangel," the Good News of Jesus Christ as God's solution to our brokenness and broken hearts. Evangelicals should be people who embody this Good News, passionate people whose uncontainable joy confirms and invites others to seek God's gift, God's answer, the irresistible Christ of God.

Despite a widespread stereotype, evangelical is not a far-right political party. When we appear to be, we deny our identity and betray our purpose. Christ-following evangelicals are not looking to take control. Quite the opposite.

Evangelicals, who are captivated by the Kingdom of God, will submit ourselves to the sacred agenda and spiritual discipline of love, joy, peace, patience, kindness, goodness, faithfulness, gentleness and self-control...that wins by losing, that gains by giving ourselves, that leads by serving. That becomes Good News to everyone who is drawn by the selflessness, generosity and sheer joy of such an all-inclusive appeal.

The Gospel, this Good News, makes it possible to live a joy-driven life from a platform of gratitude. Under any circumstances, adverse or favorable. This conviction is anchored in the unfolding story of the Bible and can be sustained in the face of the worst threats. And is, incidentally, the best strategy for mental health and human flourishing.

Steve Kerr is the head coach of the Golden State Warriors, an NBA basketball team that has earned tremendous success over the past few years and won the admiration of a vast swath of fans. Coach Kerr teaches his players to play by four core values. The preeminent is: joy.

Say again?! Professional sports is incredibly competitive, is a cutthroat business, exacts a physical, emotional and relational toll on athletes with a limited career in view. Exactly!

So Coach Kerr insists that his team enjoy the journey, have fun, believe in the plan and in your teammates, believe that mistakes are not fatal, that a bad game is not a tragedy, that we can learn from every experience and bounce back. Believe it and rejoice in every situation—whether challenging or rewarding.

Kind of has a biblical ring to it.

Joy is what we want, what we need, what gets us moving, what prevents us from giving up. It is the underappreciated virtue that has the power to bind us together. It is not a psychological ploy to motivate us, it is an awakening to the reality of God's intention to bless us, an experience of his incredible goodness, a beautiful by-product of our renewed relationship with the God who showers us with pure love.

Don't try to manufacture this or conjure it up. God finds you wherever you are (shepherds huddled in their fields, for example) and wows you with it. With the soul-stirring sensation of knowing the one, true, living God.

Imagine that. I hope you can.

Gifted

Yes, it hits you, coming out of left field, seemingly. CS Lewis recalls being "surprised by joy." And the direction of his life, the reason for his existence, was changed forever. It was this intervention that opened his mind and heart to a much larger and much more engaging reality.

"It would seem that our Lord finds our desires not too strong, but too weak. We are half-hearted creatures, fooling about with drink and sex and ambition when infinite joy is offered us, like an ignorant child who wants to go on making mud pies in a slum because he cannot imagine what is meant by the offer of a holiday at the sea. We are far too easily pleased."

But you must choose his gift. We must open our wounded, suspicious, faithless, locked-down hearts. We have to humble ourselves, relinquish our failed strategies for happiness and give in to the joy that awaits us.

Jesus splashes us with joy when he comes near and we dare to stay close, to bask in the drenching. We learn to live overwhelmed by his grace and liberating truth, and live always in anticipation of the next joy-filled development as we follow him. We keep it fresh and stay resilient by always staying connected to the Source.

Author and caregiver Henri Nouwen put it this way. "There is a lot of old pain, old sadness, old grief...but there is no such thing as old joy. Joy is always new." We don't live from a legacy, or conforming to a tradition, or by borrowing the faith of someone else. We must find our own direct real-time relationship with God and discover for ourselves the Jesus of Bethlehem who is now the Risen Christ, and this revitalizing joy he offers.

As we mature in our spiritual walk we realize that pain and joy come in the same package. If you don't want the pain, you don't get the joy. And then we generate accommodating delusions that we hope will help us survive because we don't know how to handle the contradictions.

We have to live in denial or fabricate comforting fantasies. Because, obviously, joy and pain can't coexist!

But authentic joy is so strong it can hold the pain, it can frame and re-position the pain, and ultimately transform it. Joy recognizes God's ability to work despite and around—as well as in and through—the suffering to produce inconceivable blessing and benefit. If in our weakness God's strength can blast through, if in our poverty God enriches us, if suffering can lead to the refining of character...and if God is already crafting a future of perfect justice and peace...we can relax and enjoy, as we weep and pray and work, while wars rage.

Sure. How we wish it were it true. It still seems like the impossible dream.

The Longest Night

Life has a way of dashing our dreams and deconstructing our hope.

Can this offer of joy override the daily grind, can it withstand threats, can it face down tragedy...can it defeat death? If it can't (and, of course, it can't, because nothing can) then we appreciate the sentiment and the respite, and the effort to lift our spirits.

But we are grown-ups now, wary of fairy tales, hardened by tough times, and left with a single existential option...bravely resigning ourselves to the inevitability of the end. The end of life, of relationships, of happiness, of all we now hold dear, of every sweet fleeting dream. There is no such thing as joy that lasts. Sorry.

Late one October night, a number of years ago, my sister was killed in a car crash. My Dad woke us up with the terrible news. It's the dreaded call nobody wants to get. By the time I heard, she was gone.

We had to wake up her 19 year-old daughter who had just moved in with us and tell her. My sister was divorced, so there was no father nearby. We were her only family, her brother away at college.

Our hurting family would spend the rest of the night together, mostly quiet, lost in our sad thoughts. It was a very long night.

Early in the morning I called the high school where my sister was a teacher. I told them what had happened and asked if I could come and tell her classes in person. The principal and the district superintendent both escorted me from one classroom to the next where I shared the bad news. I felt like I was in a trance. I appreciated their support. They never interrupted me, even when I talked about our faith.

I wanted these teenagers to know how much their teacher loved them. What I didn't know was how much they loved her. She was the teacher who wouldn't let anyone flunk, not if she could help it. She would spend extra time with any kid who was close to the edge and would help them improve their grade. They grieved the loss along with me. By the end of the day, I was exhausted.

We held the memorial service and a hundred kids from her school came, bearing a giant poster with messages from themselves and others. So many expressions of love, so much sorrow, leaving us feeling empty. Not a sliver of joy in sight, none that I could see. Even with the standard references to "a better place."

Finished with the formalities, we settled into a new and diminished world without Kathi. I didn't like it.

For one, I felt like I had failed. I'm the big brother. I'm supposed to be watching out for my younger siblings. In fact, I had involved myself before when she was in trouble. That's my job. I also remembered when I was not the caring brother I was supposed to be. I don't think I ever compensated her for that.

I carried the anxiety with me. Words intended to comfort me, as drive-by encouragement, almost had the opposite effect. I couldn't pull out of this agitation, this depression. And I almost never get depressed.

It was a couple of months later, and I was stuck. Preferring to withdraw when I could. There must be some way to fix it, but there's not. That was a frustration every day, as my mind would imagine a retroactive rescue scenario...with me as the champion who arrives just in time.

Then one night I had a dream. Now I'm not a mystic, I'm a man of action. What can I do to make a difference here?! That's my reaction, that's how I'm wired.

It is interesting how visions and dreams are prominent as signs in the Bible, pointing toward the hidden activity of God. God can and will do whatever it takes to get through to us.

In my dream I was transported to heaven (which is a big surprise all by itself...absent God's mercy). I'm in heaven, or some idyllic picture of heaven, but I'm not happy. I'm in no mood to join with the raucous throngs who are celebrating their arrival.

I'm here to find Him. I've got questions. He's the only one who can give me the answers I need. I'm tired of people telling me there are no answers.

Finally, I see him in the distance, out in a meadow, surrounded by his good friends I suppose, having a great time...for some reason. I rush to catch up (hard to do in a dream) and when I do, I push everyone else aside and get right up in his face.

There is no time for introductions or an exchange of pleasantries. As in, "Thank you for letting me into your heaven! It's really nice here!"

I get as close as I dare to him and let loose with a barrage of questions and accusations. Without warning or preamble I begin my rehearsed interrogation. I start loud and get louder. My anger is unrestrained. I pour out my anguish.

"My sister died, and you could have stopped it. She was cut down in the prime of her life. Her children need her, her students adore her, she has so much more to give. If you were too busy to save her, you could have told me and I would have been there and stopped this from happening. I would have done anything. There must have been something you could have done, but you did nothing. And we are now stuck with this agony..."

The whole time in this confrontation, in my dream, he is looking at me. With pure compassion. I recall that expression. How I resent it right now! I wanted nothing of his solicitous concern, his soft sympathy—I needed answers, something definite, something to absolve him, and assuage my conscience, and make sense of my sister's senseless death. And I wasn't going to leave until he threw me out.

My voice finally trailed off as he lifted his hands as if to slow me down, his face still transfixed with an unnerving empathy.

"I will take all the time you need to answer all the questions you have. But first, I have a question for you."

Oh God, he's doing it again. I hate it when he answers a question with a question. He's always doing that in the Gospel accounts. Refusing to answer, putting someone on the spot, turning the tables.

But now I'm on his turf. I've got to play his game. Nobody gets to challenge his rules.

"OK," I conceded. "What's your question..." A long, drawn-out sigh of exasperation followed.

My eyes are down, my very remote hope for an epiphany all but gone. The only rebel allowed into heaven, temporarily, is about to get crucified for his insubordination. I probably had it coming. And I tried to guess what his question might be.

"You have no idea what you're talking about...and anyway who are you to crash the gates of heaven and embarrass me in front of my friends? How dare you! You can go to hell."

I deserved that, but that's not what he said to me. Or, how about...

"Before I answer your silly questions, why don't we talk about your sins, and your character flaws, and all the ways you have failed me over your lifetime—you pitiful excuse for a human being—after all the blessings I've given to you!"

I didn't get that either.

Interrupting my own torrent of speculations, I looked up at him again and in a quieter, somewhat humbler voice repeated myself. "I'm ready, Lord. What's your question?" I steeled myself for the rebuke that was surely coming.

And Jesus said...

"Do you want to see her?"

As a shock wave of heavenly grace shook my whole body, he turned and gestured off into the distance where my beautiful sister is dancing, as she loved to do, and moving toward us.

And then I woke up.

In the darkness, buried by despair, out of answers, we are surprised by joy. Not just an assurance of survival. But a guarantee (strong word!) of victory in the middle of the struggle. His victory, and therefore ours.

When and where God shows up, and we wake up, there is joy. The deep settled conviction that God is for us, no matter the forces arrayed against us, no matter the mess we have made. His forgiveness secured by Christ's Cross opens the way, and Christ's Resurrection from the dead powers us on our way. Our willingness to trust this God secures his promise and eternal life begins on this day.

Too Much Trauma

One of the most intriguing and excruciating novels I have ever read is The Shack by Paul Young. Self-published as a gift to his family and close friends, this hard-hitting story has sold millions of copies over the past decade or so.

I probably have had more conversations with non-Christians about this book than any other, except the Bible itself. Because they don't think of it as religious literature. So their defenses against religious propaganda are down. It strikes most people as a book about life—about a convergence that is at once unbearable and irresistible.

The book begins with an atrocity that would destroy any normal person. Life is over if this ever happens. The patient may persist in a spiritually vegetative state but life with the possibility of meaning and joy is almost certainly over.

What if?!

What if, the book proposes...What if God invited you to bring your crushing burden to him and spend the day with him at the scene of the tragedy, unleashing all of your questions and pain and fear and rage and doubt and despair? In an intimate, no-holds-barred, extended and untimed, one-on-one (or one-on-three) conversation with the GOD of the universe?!

Wouldn't that impossible privilege, becoming possible, be amazing?!

It turns out that we do get to choose joy. We get to choose the one relationship that awakens us to the love our heart endlessly, restlessly longs for. Instilling the joy that spontaneously erupts from broken hearts, and cannot be stolen.

This is the Good News of Great Joy for all the people. The birth of Jesus into a dysfunctional world filled with ominous curses and demoralizing conflicts, launching a revolution of reconciliation and disbursing otherworldly joy on earth as the Gospel goes out.

Allowing us to live...are you listening!...with anticipation instead of apprehension, with courage instead of complacency. Under any conditions, for a lifetime...which lasts forever.

Under the influence of joy, a supernatural high requiring no artificial stimulants, filled and thrilled by the Spirit, you and I are at our best. In love with life and poised to bless anyone we meet. A vibrant and convincing illustration of the river of living water flowing out of those who follow Jesus, who is that fountain of joy.

Pope Francis, who has apparently caught the virus, puts it like this, "Instead of imposing new obligations, Christians should appear as people who wish to share their joy." Who cannot help but share their joy because we are immersed in it, marinating in it, recalibrated by it for reclamation projects of all kinds. Obsessed with the outrageous but now unshakable conviction that God will not withhold any good thing from us.

This is evangelistic joy and it's nearly irresistible.

Revelling

Reading Ephesians One through the lens of joy, and without the distortion of doubt, we ride with the Apostle Paul to the heights and revel in our preposterous privilege...

Praise be to the God and Father of our Lord Jesus Christ, who has blessed us in the heavenly realms with every spiritual blessing in Christ...He chose us in him before the creation of the world to be holy and blameless...

In love he predestined us for adoption to sonship through Jesus Christ...to the praise of his glorious grace, which he has freely given us in the One he loves...

In him we have redemption through his blood, the forgiveness of sins, in accordance with the riches of God's grace that he lavished on us.

The shock of it all never wears off. But must always be renewed.

Joy, impossible joy is ours, in our profoundly personal connection with Christ.

Joy—intimate, immense and uplifting—is ours to give away, as those around feel the effect, and wonder whether it is true and might possibly be available to them. And we leave no doubt that it is, despite all the evidence to the contrary in enemy-occupied territory that denies the Good News.

Starter Fluid

Joy as the source of life is primal. It comes first. And it is the blast at the end, and never comes to an end.

Joy is the unrestrained delight God takes in creation (*God saw all that he had made, and it was very good*), in salvation, his re-creation (*there is rejoicing in the presence of the angels of God over one sinner who repents*), and in the consummation of history that will overrule death and mourning and crying and pain and tears, and fulfill his restorative purpose (*He who was seated on the throne said, "I am making everything new!"*).

In the magisterial, multi-volume Theological Dictionary of the New Testament, the ultimate authority on the interpretation of biblical Greek, the word for grace (*Xaris*), an essential theological word—to say the least—does not appear by itself in the table of contents. Let me say that again. Grace does not have its own separate place in this comprehensive review of all the significant New Testament terms.

That is because grace, God's unmerited favor producing our good fortune, is generated by joy (*Xara*). Grace is derivative—is subordinate to it. Joy (along with the verb to rejoice, *Xairo*) is the root word, implying that grace is the wonderful outcome when joy has its way. You've got to look up *joy* to find *grace*.

God delights in loving us, is enthusiastic about showing us extravagant mercy and his delight—the joy that God gets as he acts according to his nature—powers the spectacle of divine grace. Joy is the wild card.

God doesn't grudgingly give us grace. God is joy-driven! He loves to unleash his love, bringing us to our knees at the realization of our place in his wild, sovereign affection. Our outburst of joy in response to God's avalanche of blessing gives God his due, his glory, his eye-catching, heart-stirring witness in a weary, wasting world. And unveils our special status, precipitating another round of reverberating joy and all the works of grace it inspires.

In the Vernacular, Please

Too abstract? Of course. Joy is virtually unknown, almost inconceivable, until it is experienced. And it is most often experienced when least expected and when the sheer perversity of circumstances obscures it, opposes it, or rules it out altogether.

Dr. Luke, who carefully researched and wrote his Gospel account of the life of Christ, penned a sequel called the Acts of the Apostles. It is a compendium of dramatic experiences—of both pain and joy in a jumble. More specifically, of joy erupting in the midst of exceedingly grim conditions.

Luke spends many words on the much-admired personality of Stephen in Chapters Six and Seven.

Now Stephen, a man full of God's grace and power...a man full of faith and of the Holy Spirit...performed great wonders and signs among the people. Opposition arose, however...

Because of this vicious conspiracy, Stephen was forced to go on trial and defend himself against serious charges that could lead to his execution. Standing alone. As he began his defense, Luke shares this indelible impression of a man surrounded by determined hostility...

All who were sitting in the Sanhedrin looked intently at Stephen, and they saw that his face was like the face of an angel.

This modest but powerful man began his history lesson with these words...

Brothers and fathers, listen to me! The God of glory appeared to our father Abraham while he was still in Mesopotamia..."Leave your country and your people," God said, "and go to the land I will show you."

He talked about the extreme hardships endured by the Israelites but also the constant presence and provision of God from Abraham to Joseph, from Exodus to the encounter at Sinai, from Moses and Aaron to David and Solomon, to the prophets who predicted the coming of the Messiah. He spoke of the resistance of the people to the Law of

God, to the Spirit of God, and their rejection of the "Righteous One" that "you have now betrayed and murdered."

Every step of the way, God guided them, protected them, taking them from slavery, through the wilderness, into a land flowing with milk and honey, defeating enemies too fierce for them, convening frequent festivals of joy to commemorate all of his gifts. Calling and equipping a people who had no standing, no status, no place, no future, no hope, no joy, no freedom, no food, no water, no weapons, no wealth, no leader, no inclination to live as people singled out for blessing and a world-transforming mission.

Their impossible pilgrimage and its success stunned their pagan neighbors, introduced a chaotic world to the beauty and order of ethical monotheism, and promised a marvelous multiethnic kingdom of unimagined joy.

Stephen the servant of the nascent church and a prophet to his own people laid it out. Look what He did—this "God of Glory!" See how blind you are today—you who do not perceive and will not receive the greatest gift!

The confidence of the man, the forcefulness of his words, and the favor of God above him guarded his integrity and steadied him to speak the uncompromising truth in full view of these seething critics itching for a lynching. What drives someone under extreme pressure to stay strong, to stay the course whatever the outcome?

Stephen felt the fury of the tribunal and the gathered crowd. His luminous presence was an insult and an affront to them. They had turned the story of the God who does not live in temples made by human hands into a tale of a tribal deity controlled by a highly-regulated religious institution that has abandoned grace and exiled joy.

When they picked up rocks to stop his speech...

Stephen, full of the Holy Spirit, looked up to heaven and saw the glory of God, and Jesus standing at the right hand of God. "Look," he said, "I see heaven open and the Son of Man standing at the right hand of God."

A beatific vision in the shadow of hatred, refusal and revenge. Impossible, a contradiction without resolution...as far as we're concerned. But Jesus, who is always described as sitting at the right hand of the Father, stands in honor of Stephen, ready to welcome him home.

While they were stoning him, Stephen prayed, "Lord Jesus, receive my spirit." Then he fell on his knees and cried out, "Lord, do not hold this sin against them." When he had said this, he fell asleep.

The intensity of this experience, the privilege of representing the God of Abraham, Isaac and Jacob, and the awareness of a Savior eager to receive him sent a shudder of joy through this man who was now ready to release his tormentors from the guilt of their crime...even as he was anticipating the next moment in heaven.

For the kingdom of God is not a matter of eating and drinking, but of righteousness, peace and joy in the Holy Spirit, because anyone who serves Christ in this way is pleasing to God and receives human approval.

That approval may be postponed but ultimate vindication is assured. The martyrs who choose joy beyond the safety of disinterest or disloyalty will be honored by a following that counts the cost but, like their role model, pursues the far greater reward.

Dear friends, do not be surprised at the fiery ordeal that has come on you to test you, as though something strange were happening to you. But rejoice inasmuch as you participate in the sufferings of Christ, so that you may be overjoyed when his glory is revealed.

Faith's Fixation

Therefore, since we are surrounded by such a great cloud of witnesses, let us throw off everything that hinders and the sin that so easily entangles. And let us run the race marked out for us, fixing our eyes on Jesus, the pioneer and perfecter of our faith.

For the joy set before him he endured the cross, scorning its shame, and sat down at the right hand of the throne of God. Consider him who endured such opposition so that you will not grow weary and lose heart.

The Bethlehem shepherds collided with joy in the middle of a silent night and raced to meet the Messiah in his straw crib. At the convergence of heaven and earth.

You couldn't ask for anything more. Not at Christmas. Starting a celebration that never ends. Guaranteed. *Joyeux Noel.*

You have His Word on it. You have His Son. He has you.

Moving one reformed killjoy to exclaim...
Rejoice in the Lord always. I will say it again (and again and again): Rejoice!

The Challenge

Joy and pain come in the same package. If you don't want the pain, you don't get the joy. In fact, they coexist in a constrained symbiosis, not cancelling each other out. And, it is only because of the joy that you and I can endure and process and carry the pain.

Experiencing pain offers us the opportunity to learn empathy for others in similar circumstances. As we come alongside them and are able to establish a rapport due to the fellowship of suffering, we are both surprised by the joy and the courage that emerges as each of us resonates—beyond a surface sympathy—with the experience of the other. Suffering is bonding, especially if we can detect a redemptive purpose at work. Our conversation is therapeutic and a new season of previously unimagined healing appears on the horizon.

The Experiment

1. Read Genesis 37-50 (the trials, traumas, tragedies and triumph of Joseph)

2. What setback have you survived? How did you recover? Where was God? Take a page or two and write your story.

3. What pain do you currently carry? Do you have enough joy to energize you? Take this question, and the anxiety that comes with it, to a trusted (mature, wise and caring) friend and share the weight of your burden. What are you missing? Where is the living Christ? What if anything blocks your awareness, reduces your confidence, drains your joy?

4. Dare to live this week fully aware of all the pain and all the joy—inside you and around you. Ask a friend to actively support you in this experiment. At the end of each day this week, write down what you noticed. Where was God?

CHRIST INCOGNITO

PART THREE

No Eye Has Seen

CHRIST INCOGNITO

NINE

Rumors of a Resurrection

You will seek me and find me
When you seek me with your whole heart
I will be found by you
[Jeremiah 29]

My friends and I left church on a crisp Sunday afternoon one Fall to play some touch football. But we had to make a plan because our beloved 49ers (back in the day when they had a championship football team) were in a big game on TV at the same time. So, somebody would have to record the game and we would all gather at his house to watch it later.

We were all set. Best of both worlds. Play it, watch it, perfect.

After our friendly scrum I jumped into my car, heading to the house. We had been sternly warned not to listen to any news about the Forty-Niners game so we could watch it as if it were live.

But I did what I almost always do when I start the car without thinking—I punched the radio. And, before I could turn it off, I heard the score of the game that had ended minutes earlier. Just the score, and the 49ers had won.

Should I still go and watch the replay with my buddies? I thought about it and decided to go anyway, not realizing how complicated this would become.

In the first half, the Niners were dreadful. Nothing worked. Joe Montana could not connect with his receivers, Jerry Rice(!) dropped a pass that hit him in the hands, and the running game was completely ineffective. They were down by two touchdowns at halftime.

Some of the guys were even talking about leaving. It certainly looked like a lost cause. I gently encouraged them to stick it out. "You never know," I said knowingly, "they might come back. You wouldn't want to miss that."

"Highly unlikely," one of them shot back. "It's painful to watch." But they stayed—for the food and the camaraderie more than for the useless efforts of our team.

Small consolation as the game went grinding on. Lots of moaning and groaning and complaining in the room. Nobody held back from expressing their bitter disappointment and tortured despair as the third quarter wore on without any consolation or tangible hope. Except me.

It was a strange place to be. I had heard the score and knew they were going to win. But nothing I was watching supported that certainty. It looked bad.

But I was intrigued. Paying attention when the others kept turning away. How are they going to pull this out?

I felt great empathy for my friends. I would be seriously depressed, as well, if I was taking all of this in without benefit of the news I had heard. News that made me frequently shake my head in disbelief as the plot unfolded—that then re-energized me for the next sequence of plays as I scoured the scenes with great interest for signs of a possible breakthrough.

Near the end of the third quarter, the 49ers finally scored. The room erupted. Me, not so much, though I was very pleased. I was expecting this. I told you so, I wanted to say out loud.

The fourth quarter was pure drama. Everybody was on a roller coaster racked by the severest doubt. A zig-zag, crazy-making ride of agony and ecstasy, and then back to the free fall of utter despondency. It's so much fun to watch this ridiculous game! Not as much fun if all of this actually mattered.

Sometime in the fourth quarter, after Roger Craig fumbled (again), one of my best friends started staring at me. "What's with you, Stevens?"

he asked from across the room. "Don't you care what happens?" So much passion in his voice. Almost a plea.

I just smiled, a little sheepishly. "I've been watching you," he said, apparently a bit perplexed. "You're not affected by this like you should be." He's shaking his head. "Do you know something the rest of us don't know? Huh?!"

Busted.

I looked back at him—as everybody else was looking at me during this commercial break, searching for the truth. I had no words. Not yet.

"Hey..." There was an awkward pause. "Dude, you must have heard the final score! *Did you hear the score?*" he demanded. When I didn't deny it he rushed across the floor, a look of semi-serious indignation on his face, and drove me deep into the couch with a flying tackle.

Though the game wasn't over, and our team was still behind, and it pretty much seemed futile based on their performance so far...everyone now knew the outcome. Somehow, San Francisco will find (had found) a way to win this game. It's a foregone conclusion. *This* explains Doug's unusual, out-of-synch demeanor.

Hmmm.

This, of course, is the situation we find ourselves in as we navigate life in this world. But it's no game. It's literally a matter of life and death. And, as we all know, death wins. Hints of our eventual demise are everywhere.

But we are the people who have heard the final score, we have read ahead. We know that God has won the victory over sin and death and the powers of evil.

We know from history, we know by faith, we know by experience, we know because we have God's Word on it and because the character of God secures our trust. We know because Jesus Christ, the crucified one, who was dead, is alive again and promises Life—eternal life (beginning as soon as it dawns on us), super-abundant life in the here and now, and life neverending in a new heaven and new earth—to all who believe.

If Jesus was raised from the dead, as the New Testament claims...
If the future hope of the Resurrection has invaded this present age...
If that same power has been unleashed in the lives of those who put their trust in the Risen One...
If we can absolutely count on the Return of the Risen Christ to set things right...

What practical, perspective-altering, life-changing difference does this make in your everyday world?

We should be living in the awareness of this new reality, this secret meant to be widely, indiscriminately shared. This changes our whole perspective because this changes everything!

People should be asking us:
What is with you? (Or, really: *Who* is with you?!)
How can you be at peace? Where does *that* come from? Why aren't you afraid?

How can you have such hope in the middle of this mess?

Where are you finding the joy when life is falling apart?

How can you still believe when life is so hard?

How can you afford to be so honest, so unselfish, so generous, so loving, all the time?

Why aren't you playing the lottery?

People should be asking us every day about our unusual attitude that defies the typical interpretations of circumstances and the manic-depressive implications of experience in an uncertain, out-of-control world.

We don't have to do a lot of preaching, a lot of telling, a lot of correcting (and no shaming, no condemning). Simply a lot of grace-filled, joy-driven living...in light of the shocking Resurrection...under the headline of an undying hope this Best News Ever installs over our everyday lives.

The Challenge

Joy is aroused by our perception of the retroactive intrusion of Good News from the future into the present in such a way that our whole perspective changes, our entire paradigm shifts, all sadness and doubts and despair are confronted. The presence of Christ in our world signaled the beginning of the Age to Come, a time of fulfillment promised to the people of God centuries earlier. What Christ accomplished in his life and ministry, death and resurrection, ascension to heaven and gifting of the Spirit certifies that the end of an old worn out, broken down era has arrived—yielding to the new creation reality of affirmation and transformation, grace and forgiveness, abundance and generosity, service and sacrifice, faith and courage, reckoning and reclamation, all directed by and suffused with an otherworldly love come down to us on earth.

This is all a mystery, at first, because the Kingdom of God infiltrates the systems of this world and may seem impotent by secular standards. But the Gospel is an open secret and the restored world that God intends is already present as a preview of what is certainly to come. That will someday fill the earth when Christ is acclaimed as the rightful King, the Prince of Peace, the Champion of Humankind. No longer Christ incognito.

The Experiment

1. What does all of this mean to you?
2. Read Hebrews 1 and 2; also 8 – 10
3. If you knew you could not fail, and that no amount of op-position or discouragement mattered, what would you do, what would you give your life for?
4. Make a plan. Be specific about doing one thing. Be as bold as your joy enables.

TEN

Spirited Away

White Water Rafting Without the Raft

Worry is a Mild Form of Atheism

"You want to body surf it?" he asked with a nod to the river, an apparent twinkle in his dark brown eyes. I did a quick study of his face for any hint that he was spoofing me. You've got to be kidding! As in... man-overboard, good-luck, go-for-it, we'll be searching for your water-logged remains in some quiet eddy downstream?! I don't think so.

We had just survived a rollicking raft ride through the churning rapids known as "Riptide"—the last stretch of white water on our perilous journey down the east fork of the Salmon River in Central Idaho. It was great fun and demanded a coordinated effort as we threaded our way around the treacherous rocks, over the steep falls into the swirling maelstrom below, and onward as our constantly contorting rubber raft careened down a roller coaster chute that eventually spilled into calmer waters. Rafting the river took the skill of our guide, all the muscle of our six-person crew, and considerable courage as we confronted a primordial power much greater than ourselves.

And now the guide who leads the whole caravan of river runners is asking me—do I want to surf it, without the benefit of a boat? By the way, is this even legal?

I'm slow to respond, taking a couple of extra seconds. Well, all right, if you're serious. Let's do it. Um, are you sure it's OK? What's it like?

I grabbed my buddy Steve who enthusiastically, if somewhat mindlessly, consented and we followed our dauntless guide as he led us on a slow scramble back over the boulders that lined the riverbank to an inlet above the roaring rapids. Of course, some very practical questions would have to be suppressed for the time being. We could coolly assess the situation as we went, and certainly back out of it if we didn't feel comfortable. But we should at least look at it. Couldn't hurt.

Somehow, from this new vantage point standing knee-deep in the river, the headlong rush of the water in front of us—cascading, spiraling, dropping—seemed faster, more voluminous, much louder and much closer than before. It seemed almost alive. More than a match for the human twigs about to throw ourselves into the ceaseless, thunderous flow. Warning us away and, at the same time, strangely, compelling us to come in.

Our composed guide waded out ahead of us into the clear, swift-running river. He was moving purposely—we were moving cautiously behind him, falling farther behind with each step, trying to brace ourselves, to secure a tentative balance. So far, so good, I thought as we watched him reach the middle, eyes forward, arms spread out, a portrait of total concentration.

For me this was still only a preview of a wild and increasingly remote possibility from a safe distance—not yet the reality of the unimaginably violent pull and relentless pounding we would undoubtedly experience if we dared to follow. Let's watch and see, I said wordlessly, as I glanced back at my wide-eyed partner on this trek off the grid.

Our guide was motionless in the middle of the river for a suspended moment, scanning the tumult awaiting us. And then...he let go, allowing the river to take full control. Feet in front, gnarly tennis shoes his only defense against any obstacle that rose up to assault him downstream. Lying on his back, buoyed by his life jacket, undulating with the uneven flow, how could he see what was coming at him and prepare for the worst?

A high-pitched yelp—was it terror or joy?—and he was gone. Almost immediately he was a speck bobbing in the current, and then he disappeared altogether. We couldn't hear him and, in all the soup and foam, we lost visual contact.

This looks very bad, we both thought, and simultaneously agreed that we needed to beat a hasty retreat to the shore to reconsider this insanity. Did you see how the river just took him?! Our growing anxiety gave us away.

I immediately tried to turn around. But it was too late. The decision to wade into the water was the last one I got to make. Without realizing it, I had already gone too far, past some invisible point of no return. Almost as soon as I contemplated getting out, the river picked me up.

When Steve saw me upended by the sudden, irresistible surge he assumed I had intended to take the plunge, and he didn't want to be left behind. And so, both of us, ready or not, were now on our irreversible way.

I screamed, inaudibly. Find the bottom, hold on to something, stop yourself! But the reckless race into an unfathomable future was on. If I had a future.

All I could think about was getting thrashed. Thoroughly. A human pin ball slamming into rocks and branches and random debris above and below the water line. I was fighting every inch of progress toward the frothy inferno I knew was imminent.

This can't be happening, I pleaded. I can't believe the power! I am nothing. The power is everything. I am...a dead man.

Beneath me, the lush underwater landscape is a shimmering, fast-vanishing blur, an eerie distortion of depth and distance. Miraculously, I miss the granite monolith rising as an impassable barrier in the center of this rampaging expressway. I sideswipe a second rock...not as large but sharper. Then, in a sea of furious agitation, I am over the edge of a waterfall and into the vortex of a voracious abyss.

As I sail over the liquid precipice I catch sight of a spectacle so threatening—and so impressive—that I despair of trying to describe it. Maybe this is heaven; maybe this is hell.

Overlooking a frothy cavernous void, I confront a fulminating upheaval of white-washed water rising up on the other side. Whether this pulse-pounding instant will be death-dealing or life-changing, I don't know.

This is the river at its most raging, with a master mind and determination of its own. It means to take me down, I am convinced, to override me, to overrule any contrary conviction I might vainly possess.

Then, after spouting its drastic dominance, it buries me under a dense torrent of waves—drowning my cries, denying my preference for peace, obliterating my awareness of the world around. Still fighting...I stop fighting. And in that submission I tendered my resignation. I accepted the river's terms for unconditional surrender.

I was gone! Forcibly submerged despite my life vest—with no ability to resist or maneuver or even protest. With no sense of where I was or where I was going or what might become of me. Helpless, carried along, crazily spinning, tightly gripped by the river I never expected to know so intimately.

Afraid to die, afraid to keep going, unable to breathe, afraid to hope, afraid to let go—though I already had, and afraid somehow of missing something amazing along the way. So afraid, and afraid of my fear, I abandoned all pretense of being able to contend with anything that was happening. In my state of relaxed panic, I gave up...and gave in to the momentum...as a curious tourist, as an avid explorer, as a zealous devotee.

As if in response to a desperate prayer, I was thrust back up through the surface...shot from nowhere, improbably skimming across the slick surface, jet-propelled. Hyper-ventilating now, I felt an overwhelming exhilaration. Abandoning every security I had ever relied upon, I had been seized and held hostage by an intractable energy, by a commanding urgency.

Catapulted through a timeless, boundary-less, horizon-less panorama, I was hurled against my severest doubts. Some force—or some One— with a plan to accelerate my life, to elevate my spirit, pinned wings on this reluctant downhill swimmer. Fly or die! Sink or swoon... enchanted by the effortless motion.

God, this is great! I exclaimed with a whisper. This is so great!

I writhed and frolicked in the subsiding surf like a carefree child. Unrepentantly gleeful. Slowing down by now but still mesmerized by the preternatural power, by the ferocious flow of untamed energy... by this foray into uncharted territory...by the midday madness and the mystery that infused a sudden, serene and unexplained confidence.

Giddy with delight, I washed ashore. I could not subdue the high hilarity that lit up my face. I flopped and floundered in the shallows, unavoidably impaled on a bolt of happiness, absorbed in this delicious memory.

I had lived through the ordeal, living again because of it. I had inadvertently broken into another dimension. Figuring I lost everything by foolishly following—my timid, derivative faith was rewarded with an adventure I would never forget, from which I would never recover. Shanghaied, inundated, captivated, liberated, released and transformed.

I finally remembered to wonder how my fellow travelers had fared. They must be all right. I was quite certain. They must be sprawled on the beach, somewhat delirious like me, musing over the secret of the river.

About fifty feet downstream Steve was sitting perfectly still, arms draped over bent knees, staring, beaming. Absolutely drained and yet obviously renewed. Wrung out and, like me, revitalized. We had both run the grueling gauntlet, danced with demons, rescued by angels, and thrilled by the sheer audacity of our dangerous, defiant descent into the heavenlies.

We babbled on incoherently about the un-navigable course and our impossible success...until a familiar figure, our ghostly guide with some apparent amusement interrupted our impromptu celebration. At first sight, we didn't know whether we wanted to hug him or inflict grievous pain on his much-too-resilient river-ravaged body.

After some minutes of male bonding, he reissued the outrageous invitation. "Want to run it again?" he offered, almost nonchalantly, a not-so-innocent twinkle in his bloodshot eyes.

"What?!" Where does this guy get his nerve? We looked at each other and then back at this smiling provocateur. "Yeah, sure, why not?! What an incredible ride! What a rush! I almost died.

How big a drop-off is that waterfall? Does anyone ever get trapped in the whirlpool? How long were we under water? Has anyone ever attempted this besides us?"

We never stopped talking as we portaged ourselves around the bend for another heart-starting free-fall through liquid space. We couldn't believe we were agreeing to do this again. We knew better. And we knew we could not pass up the next chance of a lifetime.

Full of trust, full of apprehension, brimming with anticipation, and as much as humanly possible ready to take the double-dare, we plunged a second time into the once forbidding, forever inviting, restless, raucous, rapturous, runaway river.

God invites us to step into the river—and we don't want to go. Even though we do. Everything in us resists. And yet, at the same time, we are drawn. We are intrigued. The river is invigorating even as its length is frequently punctuated with danger. My life might end if I go in; it might never start if I don't. Such a dilemma!

The river represents life lived as a great journey of radical discipleship, a journey replete with struggle and joy. This is God's will pictured in a vivid, soul-stirring metaphor—that is even more dramatic than the physical ordeal.

It takes great faith to step into the flow. Where it will lead and how it will go, we cannot know in advance. All we know for certain is Who it is we're following, Who is shaping and training and watching over us. And we don't know everything about Him—not yet. It gets even better as we do, and even harder, and more demanding, and more meaningful.

The first step of faith from the secure bank into the water is a small one. But most meaningful, an eventful launch. The first step may seem insignificant, as we are still filled with fear, but it is already the beginning of the expedition. The first steps take us into a new environment and under the control of a force much greater than ourselves. We are already following, timid though we may be. Putting ourselves under the influence, into a realm of new possibilities.

The river runs at its own pace, not ours. It picks us up and takes us wherever it goes. There are identified obstacles along the way and uncharted underwater hazards. But there is ecstasy, there is beauty, the thrill of immersion, the sweet camaraderie of traveling companions, the wonder of trust—the most necessary, most life-giving and life-threatening experience in the universe.

Trust? How can I? There's so much at stake. Too much, and I'm afraid of what I might have to face, what I might risk, what I might lose.

And if I can't, or I won't...I will stay stuck right where I am, glued to the ground, reclining in my luxury lounge chair on the beach, unwilling and unable to move, far away from my destiny. How sad is that?! Like so many people...spectators on the sidelines. Unchallenged, unresponsive, spectacularly unfulfilled. Critical of those who take the plunge.

Follow me, Jesus says. *Let go and let's go! Trust me! Trust me with your life! Learn to trust me every day on the road, on the river, in the wilderness, on top of a mountain or down in a crevasse, in all sorts of unsettled circumstances.*

When they did, his first disciples moved with him, witnessed miracles, absorbed life lessons, got traction, gained momentum, became like the One they kept on tracking.

Read Matthew Chapter 4, verses 12 through 17. *A light has dawned... the Kingdom of God has come near!* Then read verses 18 through 22. His first followers are called and leave the familiarity, comforts and customary agendas of their previous places and embrace a new identity, heading in a new direction, owning a new vocation. Finally, read verses 23 through 25. What a wild ride! All heaven breaks loose! While hell throws a tantrum. Meanwhile, they are right in the middle of it.

Marvel at the audacious and often overlooked invitation in Luke Chapter 9, verses 57 to 62. Consider the cost, and the rewards, in each of the three encounters:

If you want to find freedom, let go of your security!
If you want to experience significance, let go of your dependency!
If you want to fulfill your mission, stop making excuses!

All as essential preparation for hearing final instructions and for anticipating the bold adventures to be launched in Luke 10. Don't miss this! Imagine joining these authorized and energized voyagers who "returned with joy" who are now insisting that "even the demons submit to us in your name."

"I will show you the most excellent way..." the Apostle Paul later writes as an enticement at the end of I Corinthians 12. *"Follow the way of love..."*

he writes at the beginning of Chapter 14, all the while practicing what he is preaching. Read all of Chapter 13, if you dare. And run that gorgeous, vertiginous stretch of the river!

John the Seer stands in awe at the end of time and pictures "the river of the water of life, as clear as crystal, flowing from the throne of God and of the Lamb down the middle of the great street of the city..." in Revelation Chapter 22 (the last in the Bible), verses 1 and 2. Flowing with inconceivable blessing, flooding all of creation, causing it to flourish and bloom.

The love of God will lift you up and spirit you away. Embrace the river...or, at least, put your big toe in, take small steps in the shallows. Watch what happens. Be forewarned! And, bon voyage!

Jesus is our experienced, completely reliable, incredibly caring guide—going ahead of us, showing us the way, because He is the way! The one who follows, who enters, who finds their way, will not be disappointed, never lost...and never bored.

The Challenge

We say we want adventure! But we put lots of conditions on it. We need to know we're going to be safe, that it won't be too hard, that we won't forfeit any of your necessary conveniences, that our overall sense of control will not be upset or disrupted in any way.

We just killed it. We don't want to go on a real adventure, we want to go on a ride at an amusement park. We want to watch other people go off on adventures from the comfort and security of our seats in a theater. With popcorn and a soda. We're all about virtual adventure.

The Experiment

1. Read Psalm 56.

2. Walk across the street, or across the campus, or across the gym, or across the...and introduce yourself to someone you don't know. Find something you have in common. Find out something significant about them. Pray about all this and see what happens.

3. Volunteer with an outreach that is doing God's work in your community. Something that you believe in but something that is not always comfortable for you. Stretch. See what happens. Ask God to show you what he wants to happen.

4. Join a small group of truth-seekers. Tell them up front that you are determined to grow in your faith. That you are restless, need their support, and want them to hold you accountable. Consider any counsel you get and let the Word be your guide. Expect challenges.

ELEVEN

Into the Fire

He is no fool who gives up what he cannot keep
To gain what he cannot lose.
[Jim Elliot]

Those who are taken captive by Jesus see mission
Not merely as a practice preferred by God
But as essential to his character.
God is mission.
[Michael Frost]

For the Spirit God gave us
Does not make us timid
But gives us boldness, love and self-discipline.
[II Timothy 1:7]

On January 8th, 2011, a very disturbed young man with a grudge (it's frightening how many there are) approached Congresswoman Gabrielle Giffords as she was hosting a friendly meet-and-greet rally at a shopping center in Tucson. He pulled out a semi-automatic pistol and fired at point blank range, striking her in the head. Then he turned the gun on others in attendance at the gathering and shot 17 people before being subdued—killing six, including a district court judge, a nine year-old girl, and an elderly man shielding his wife. Incredibly, Giffords survived though she was grievously wounded.

The nation was shocked at such senseless violence, as it has been many times since. The close-knit community in North Tucson was devastated.

I heard the terrible news on that Saturday while I was at home in the San Francisco Bay Area. It hit me particularly hard because at the time I was commuting to Tucson every month while serving as a transitional pastor in that community.

What can I do? I won't be back there for a few more days. My immediate thought, after checking in with some people from the church, was to call a good friend who was an executive at Safeway, whose storefront was the scene of the massacre.

"What are you hearing?" I asked. "Man, I am so sorry about this tragedy. How are your employees there? What are you able to do for them? Is there anything I can do—or we as the church can do? Our campus is only a couple of miles away." I wondered if the supermarket chain had a standard procedure to put into place for such an extreme situation.

"Thanks for calling," he said, surprised to hear how close I was to this awful incident. "We are already moving to take care of our employees there. We have hired a team of therapists and they will be meeting with all of those working at that store. They are pretty traumatized. The whole shopping center is now a crime scene and will be closed for a while but the staff will regroup this week."

Then he paused. "The one thing we haven't figured out is how to support our customers after we reopen and they come back to shop. Maybe you can help us with that." We brainstormed over the phone how that might happen and what could be helpful.

So, I went to work calling up those I knew in my church and in our area who I thought could handle such a sensitive situation. And, in conversations with others, began to create a response.

When the store opened one week later on a Saturday morning, we set up a table inside the store, about 20 feet directly in front of the main entrance. A sign on the front of the table simply read:

Conversations / Questions / Prayer

Two of us were in position at all times to greet people and connect with them if they were obviously anxious or seemed to be open to some sort of engagement. I scheduled myself from 7 am to Noon that day. I ended up staying until 7 pm. I couldn't leave. Almost everybody wanted to connect at some level. And it didn't take much to get the conversation going. "How are you doing?" asked with interest and empathy usually sufficed.

Many of the encounters were heart-to-heart, almost instantly. People were emotional and reflective, most wanted to talk, needed to talk with someone. Some were distraught, overwhelmed. There was an astonishing openness to speak about their most personal feelings, and hopes, and give voice to concerns and fears that could not be easily answered.

At one point a store clerk came over and asked me if I would go to a man who was inconsolable, sitting at a table outside. I quickly went to him and sat down, saying nothing for several minutes, just taking in the apparent heartache.

Finally, I put my arm around him. "Tell me how this is hurting you?" I asked in a soft tone. My question interrupted his sobbing.

"I was here last Saturday," he told me, now looking at me. "I was shopping in the store when we heard a popping sound coming from just outside. At first, I thought they were balloons popping but then somebody shouted and people started to run. So, I began to run. I was a coward! I ran as fast as I could to the back of the store. It was complete chaos. People running and screaming." He buried his head in his arms and slumped over the table.

"Running away is a natural reaction when there's a threat," I said, reacting to his confession. "Most of us do. I'm glad you were safe."

Now he turned toward me and put both hands on my arms. "But I'm such a coward," he repeated his accusation with tears slowly rolling down his face.

"But you have come back today. Tell me what drew you here." He looked away and then in a calm, much quieter voice he said, "I have a friend who works in produce and I've come to see him, to make sure he's all right. I always talk to him when I'm shopping here. I couldn't find him the other day after I panicked." And then the emotion returned. "I have to know that he's OK," he said firmly.

"I think we should go find him," I told him.

"But I can't go in there. I'm so ashamed." He couldn't go in and he wouldn't leave. His anguish was undisguised. The story of how many people in how many places?!

"Can I pray for you, my brother?" I offered, not at all certain if this was the time and the place. He bowed his head and said nothing—which I took as agreement, or acquiescence.

With my arm around him, I prayed for this immobilized man with a broken heart. That he would find the faith to move and find his friend. And show his love. That his friend inside was waiting for him and would be happy to see him. I prayed in Jesus' name, assured that he was right there with us.

"I'm not sure I can do this. Maybe I'll come back later," he half-pleaded. "I think this is the time," I countered. "I'll walk in with you. We'll go find him." And after another moment of hesitation on his part..."Let's go," I said. And we did, walking slowly at first, me gently pushing him, unsure if we were going in the right direction.

Then, as we made our way up the first aisle, he broke into a trot as he caught sight of a man stacking boxes of fruit. I couldn't keep up, and didn't need to, as I watched the two bearhug in a spontaneous reunion.

The rest of the day was like that. Lots of meaningful contact with strangers still in shock, lost in thought, processing this drama and what it meant to them, experiencing a kind of emotional vertigo and spiritual disorientation. The twelve hours I spent there that day—inside and outside the store—were exhausting and exhilarating.

There was a young Mom with her little kids asking me to explain to her children what had happened and how they should still feel safe. There was a family that had recently emigrated from a very dangerous part of the world who were caught off guard by this attack. There were people gathered outside around a makeshift memorial filling up with flowers, stuffed animals, interspersed with notes of sorrow and affection and faith. Our team was primed for a caring, respectful approach. Our usual reticence was gone.

I stepped into a circle of motorcycle gang members who had driven a long distance for the occasion. I thanked them for being there and asked if I could pray with them. Nobody said No that day. We went into a holy huddle. I was embarrassingly bold, and they were uncharacteristically humble. It worked.

I stood with a husband and wife and listened to them candidly discuss their pain, on top of the pain symbolized by this memorial. Wounds had been re-opened. Fresh pain stabbed bystanders. Unspoken fears poured out.

One man walked into the building, took one look at us at the table, and blurted out his true feelings. "Oh yeah, Safeway is gonna make a killing today," he said to no one in particular, almost laughing, apparently unaware of the offensiveness of his language. I stood up and moved toward him. I wanted to protect others from this loose cannon.

"I'm not sure what you mean..." I offered, trying to pose it as a genuine question.

"All this publicity is going to bring in a lot of business for good ol' Safeway today," he announced to everyone within earshot. "You'll probably triple your profits and make up for the money you lost this week. Quite a scam." I wanted to punch him. What an idiot. People died here! This company is doing its best to recover and keep on serving, to continue feeding this community.

"Sir, you sound upset about something but I'm not sure what it is," I said, restraining myself. He smiled in a condescending way and unleashed a cold fury at me. "Well let me ask you something...how much you getting for overtime this week? Huh?! Be honest!"

Oh, I thought to myself, *I'm so glad you asked.* "I'm a volunteer. Not getting paid for this."

Not prepared for my response, this corporate critic stopped himself. "Oh really. Well that's admirable," he conceded. Then he looked past me. "I just really don't like this place. They ripped me off once. It's left a bitter taste."

Now we're getting down to something. And we spent the next number of minutes unpacking his bad experience—and separating it from the events of the past week. He actually thanked me at the end of our initial standoff.

This was also part of my amazing day in the line of fire. As I discovered, yet again, how God shows up in the most unexpected places and in the most unexpected ways. And wants us to get caught up in his redemptive schemes. As fully vested partners. Somehow establishing rapport and discerning real needs.

During that grand reopening I was introduced to the district manager of the grocery chain who stopped by to see how we are were getting along. Of course, he expressed his thanks to me—representing the 20+ volunteers that I had recruited. Then I asked for a favor. "Anything," he said foolishly.

"I'd like you to come to our church tomorrow morning. You can give us an update on how the store is doing in the aftermath of the shooting and we can pray for you and all those you are responsible for."

"That's not going to happen, unfortunately," was his instant response. "I live in Phoenix and my wife is expecting me home tonight."

"Well, we'd love to meet your wife, too. Why don't you invite her to come down and join us at church." I wasn't sure he was convinced, so

I added, "I'm sure our congregation would be honored to hear from an exec at Safeway since so many of us buy our groceries here."

He stammered and then dialed his wife who was, according to him, ecstatic about visiting our church. "She's very religious," he said as he resigned himself to this obligation, "but I should probably warn you that the walls may fall down as soon as I enter the building. It's been a long time."

"We'll take our chances, I appreciate it."

The next day he was there and I invited him up on the platform with me. Did his wife just wink at me? "Tell us how your team is doing," I asked. "We're already praying for everybody who's been hurt by this." And he told us, explaining about the therapy provided and the support coming from those entering the store.

My turn. I asked how we can pray for him and all those involved now. Which also included the FBI agent taking the lead on this high-profile case who was a vital part of our church. As he said some more about the impact of this terrible assault we covered everything he mentioned in prayer. It was very sobering, very moving.

At the end of our time together that morning, I issued this challenge to all of us...

Go on a walk this afternoon, around your neighborhood or wherever. Walk your dog, or take a kid in a stroller, any kid, or just take a walk by yourself. Go slow when you see somebody and call out..."How are you doing?" And wait for a response. And then get into it, believing that Christ is hosting this ad hoc encounter.

That unassuming card table with the three-fold invitation scotch-taped on the front was our base of operations for three very full days in a bustling market flooded with a community in mourning and clearly agitated on that long holiday weekend. The world stopped by. We should be there.

And then we waded out into a world that was overcome by grief and plagued by uncertainty in the wake of a close-to-home apocalypse that arrived without warning on a bright Saturday morning. Conversation flowed as we were willing to override our natural inhibitions and be unselfconsciously present.

And, to extrapolate from lessons learned when time stands still, we are invited out into our world that is in perpetual crisis...with our expression of concern, an offer of love, and a visible representation of the wild idea of viable hope in the worst of circumstances.

Hey...how are you doing? Tell me and I'll listen. I want to understand.

You are not alone. You are loved just as you are, right where you are. I am with you. Christ is for you. We can trust him with anything.

What exactly are we trusting Christ for when our formerly secured world is on the verge of collapse?

For the assurance that we are not alone. That he has resources for healing and restoration to unleash. That there is an unseen and as yet unrecognized purpose that is already in progress...and it is powerful. That there is a larger story unfolding. That what we have lost is not forever lost. That justice will be done. That there will be a reckoning. That forgiveness is an option. That living by faith even now, even here—especially here and now—will be vindicated. That God's love wins and Christ will emerge from the flames, out of the ashes, up from the grave, victorious. And so will we.

So, we can afford to activate a defiant faith and move toward conflict, toward an intimidating enemy, toward the sounds of anger and pain and hopelessness—recklessly spending ourselves on the most daunting frontiers to lift the spirits of those who have lost their way and redirect them to the compelling, invigorating love of Christ.

Jesus, who is the Christ, once said, "I will build my church and the gates of hell will not prevail against it." (Matthew 16:18). Don't picture the church as a fortress and the gates of hell battering its thick defenses. Gates are defensive measures, in this case attempting to defend the realm of hell—which features the absence of God and the exclusion of God's love—against the onslaught of a church determined to release people from their captivity. This is the force that Christ idealizes in his description of a church in full-blown rebellion against a conspiracy of bad actors, the powers that be, who are pledged to degrade and confine humanity.

In other words, as followers of Christ we are not called—not allowed—to hunker down, to sit it out. We are called to—we are defined by—a life in the shape of loving service as we emulate our Christ and crash the gates of hell. Those barriers that cannot be breached, so we are led to believe, disintegrate, so we discover, as the Spirit of Christ assaults spiritual strongholds of abuse, addiction, oppression, perversion, rage, greed, prejudice, deprivation and neglect.

I was once the pastor of Hillside Covenant Church in Walnut Creek, California. I invited my new friend Farzana and her father, refugees from Afghanistan, to join us one Sunday. Next time I saw her she raved about her experience at "Hellside," as she called it. I tried to correct her but could not modify her accent.

She would often ask about "Hellside," enjoying my consternation at this preposterous pronunciation. I chuckled too until it occurred to me one day that *Hellside* is a great name for a church. A church by the side of hell, in close proximity to trouble, sacrificing comfort and convenience because we are eager to engage the enemy for the sake of those held hostage. Involving us in a daring rescue operation. Following in the footsteps of our Lord who declared that he was sent to...

Proclaim good news to the poor
Proclaim freedom for the prisoners
Proclaim recovery of sight for the blind
and to set the captives free
Proclaim the year of the Lord's favor.
[Luke 4:18, 19]

He did, and so out of love will we...

When did we see you hungry and feed you?
Or thirsty and give you something to drink?
When did we see you a stranger and invite you in?
Or needing clothes and clothe you?
When did we see you sick or in prison and
go to visit you?

Christ the King will reply,
Truly I tell you, whatever you did for one of the least of these
You did for me.
[Matthew 25:37-40]

Which brings up a touchy topic regarding the relationship between Sunday, "The Lord's Day," and the other days of the week. Between "activities at church" and the rest of our lives lived in "the real world". Between the "sacred" and the "secular". Is that split even a legitimate reading of the Bible? Eventually bringing us around to the question of worship, the church's highest calling.

What is it? When and where does it happen?

Just because we label it "worship" doesn't mean it is. I'm greatly concerned that we have formulized, ritualized and etherealized worship in ways that reduce it to a solemn obligation or an emotional outburst or a mindless routine—an event without whole-life impact.

If worship is the posture of the heart in the presence of God, then worship cannot be programmed. It cannot be scheduled. It is not limited to a certain "sacred" space. It does not automatically happen because we call a special gathering a "worship service"...and the opportunity should not be missed because we are outside of a formal religious structure. In fact, wholehearted worship translated immediately into self-giving service is our constant calling and unending privilege. It is nothing like religion.

When we recognize God for all God is worth—as creator of all that is, as final authority in all that matters, as the only redeemer of all who are hurt and broken and lost, as the one we trust with our very lives and count on to provide for our every need—we are ready to worship by offering ourselves in good faith and ordering our lives in grateful obedience to God's perfect design and loving commands.

So, how do we worship?

"In spirit and in truth," as Jesus the Messiah very simply puts it, correcting our preoccupation with a certain venue (in Jerusalem or Samaria?) or other inconsequential traditions and preferences (and partisanship in worship wars). In other words, authentic worship emerges out of the depths of who we are (it is *spiritual*) and submitted to the story of God as revealed in the Bible, culminating in the Gospel of Christ (who is himself the truth).

But what does true worship actually look like?! If you're asking about a worship etiquette, I've got nothing. But if you're hoping for a fresh glimpse of something real and full of impact, here goes.

Whether in solitude, or in the company of two or three, or meeting with a house church, or streaming into a huge auditorium with thousands, worship tunes the heart to God's presence, God's promises and God's priorities. And we hold nothing back. We abandon ourselves to worship. We become completely receptive, spontaneously expressive, leaning into healing and massively strengthened in our resolve to follow the Christ of God and his beautiful Way of Life.

We are fully present here—listening, rejoicing, weeping, singing, giving, confessing, sharing, praying, contemplating, imagining, encouraging and caring for those around us, warmly welcoming and embracing strangers.

But this is only a moment. A catalyst. There is much more to worship.

This hour plus-or-minus of worship, private or corporate, is intended to propel us into another new week of presenting our bodies, of representing heaven on earth, of extending ourselves—our energy and talents, resources and possessions, homes and hospitality, concern and compassion, knowledge and wisdom—as a living sacrifice, for a lifetime and uninterrupted lifestyle of worship that proves our hearts are on fire, and that we are poised to walk into the fire, with Jesus-modeled, Spirit-inspired love.

Without a vision for worship as our core identity and as our driving force in everyday life...without the conviction and joy it generates...“worship” becomes bland, boring, self-focused, the occasion for sanctimony, superficiality, self-righteousness and rank hypocrisy.

I am wary of that happening to me, and it does, and worried about all of us who sometimes fail to appreciate the power of God, the treasure we have in Christ, and the aching need of the world (including us!) for the splendor, justice and mercy of the King. And convinced that a deep and daring dive into worship will ignite a revolution.

The Challenge

From worship to mission (where mission becomes worship), from a declaration of faith to a demonstration of faith (when demonstration becomes declaration), from the admiration of Christ to the emulation of Christ...this is what it means to follow him, live for him, to show our adoration. This is what "Christianity" (as colonizing acculturation) and "Christendom" (a geo-political realm) and "Christians" (nominal believers who adopt a faith of minimal compliance) are missing.

The Experiment

1. Take a walk this week...a walk around the block, around your neighborhood, through a shopping center, on a bike trail. Say Hello, introduce yourself, ask a question, offer a compliment, comment on something mundane, wonder out loud about something going on in your corner of the world. Who's alone? Who's seems sad? Who's homeless? Pray before you go. Take a friend along who will augment your intentions. Are you clear about your intentions?

2. Look for ways to engage, affirm, encourage and, if at all possible, be helpful.

3. Share what happened, what you have learned, with your inner circle.

4. What are you discovering about your community that could become a ministry—beyond an occasional foray? How is Christ leading you?
5. The next time you hear about or actually see someone or some place on "fire"...go there, be there, to showcase the compassion and courage of Christ.

CHRIST INCOGNITO

TWELVE

Sabbath Rhythm

For a Lifetime of Peak Performance (without becoming performance-based)

Defiant faith, stubborn hope, fierce love and
unassailable peace
All that is necessary
Are generated by an unshakable confidence
That God in Christ cares about me, calls me,
secures me
And is powerfully at work in me

I spoke to a group of lawyers who were on retreat one weekend. An honor and a challenge to be invited to present on a topic that would be relevant to them. "Judge Not" was my first choice, but decided it might seem too confrontational. Ha!

So, what about "Sabbath Rest"? I wondered if they might be as susceptible to pressure and stress as other high-demand occupations. And find it hard to relax. I began by asking the question and virtually everyone raised their hand.

Exodus 20:8-11 records the Fourth Command of the Decalogue. Some of us can recite it. "Remember the Sabbath Day by keeping it holy. Six days you shall labor and do all your work, but the seventh day is holy to the Lord your God...for in six days the Lord made the heavens and the earth, the sea and all that is in them, but God rested on the seventh day."

Recall what happened on Day Six in the creation scheme. Humankind, made in the very image of God, the crown of creation, was fashioned and placed in the Garden. And on their first full day after they are introduced into the unfolding panorama? They rested. It all starts with a day off.

What if we could begin each day, every week, any new season of our lives—fresh, fully charged, strong, rested and ready for all the responsibilities, opportunities and struggles that are to come? What if it were God's plan for us to launch from a platform of peace? What if Sabbath was not a rigid rule (as some of us have experienced it, and resented it, and resisted it) but a healthy rhythm that powers us through all the vicissitudes of life? What if soul-rich health and soul-full wholeness were the priority and good hard work the outflow?

What if Sabbath wasn't the reward after a long degrading week that we barely survive but the gracious provision for a profitable week of worthwhile work to come?

Embracing Sabbath with this view inspires a much needed humility. Life is a gift. Receive it, revel in it, and then take on whatever comes. With this constantly reinforced appreciation we live from a baseline of gratitude.

God is in charge, we are not. None of us is indispensable. We are not supposed to be available or on duty all the time. Relieved of all messianic expectations and pretensions, forever.

We are measured by the outpouring of God's affection not by our production—even though our performance is much less conflicted and our discernment of what should be done is, paradoxically, much increased by the poise instilled as we periodically experience a centering, uplifting Sabbath.

Humility engenders honesty. We can be confident in our calling and our capability but never arrogant or controlling. We are urged to relax into our God-given identity and not try to impersonate God. Taking the Sabbath seriously saves us from ego inflation and deflation.

Embracing Sabbath is liberating. There is freedom from endless obligation. Sabbath imposes and provides boundaries. Some of us believe that we have never done enough, are never good enough. We are still trying to prove ourselves or impress somebody or quiet the critical voice on a looping tape.

Sabbath relieves us from the requirement to do it all, to be accomplished at everything. Sabbath is the antidote to exhaustion. A regular, reliable Sabbath removes the unbearable weight.

Embracing Sabbath enforces a discipline that aims at restoring us to our best self. Sabbath is a rhythm bequeathing a balance to our frantic, fragmented lives and schedules. This is an exhilarating discipline that is exceedingly difficult for many of us to adopt. It somehow feels wrong to take a step back, to punch out, to change pace and scenery. An accusation of failure is suspended over us. And yet it is vital.

I shared one of my past-times with this group of legal professionals. I assured them that in my own way I was probably on a par in terms of my competitive nature, inclination to move toward great challenges, and strange tendency to gravitate toward crisis and combat.

So, with all that intensity in my temperament and vocation, I discovered that I really do need some sort of Sabbatical release and renewal. It has become cycling.

I get out on my bike and I am in a different world. It seems like hard work in one way, pushing up and down hills on my mountain bike but it's extremely therapeutic for me. It's a perfect counterpoint in the context of assigned work. It's solitude and it smooths out the accumulating kinks in my mind-body overload.

The good news is: your Sabbath can be customized with your needs for replenishment. This mandated day of rest was made to benefit us, not the other way around. It's not an onerous, inconvenient religious obligation—it's a life-giving, spirit-reviving privilege.

The bad news is...there is no bad news. Except that you are forced to let go of your compulsive workaholic dysfunction and look to God to confirm your worth and the value of your work. You and I have to learn to stop and to say No. And risk disappointing someone.

During my presentation to this gathering of attorneys, I used one of them as an impromptu prop (which I love to do—to keep the interaction playful and relatable, and to keep me from appearing like I'm pontificating). I interrupted myself and gestured toward his cell phone that was on the table and flashing. "See," I said with a mock-scolding tone, "see how hard it is to turn off the appliances that enslave us 24/7?!"

Self-consciously he turned it face-down and just then it rang. "Oh, I have to take it," he said, half-apologetically, "it's my wife." He paused for just a second, looking at his beckoning phone and amazed at the timing of this intrusion. "She's already texted me. I'd better answer it. This is a conflict of commandments!" We all laughed as he bolted for the door, phone in hand.

And, by the way, he is a Texas State Court of Appeals Justice who was at this retreat as a guest speaker. He was a very good sport. And a wonderful illustration of how difficult it is to navigate our hyper-connected world. Sometimes you just have to go counter-cultural to stay sane.

There are at least five symptoms of failing to embrace God's command to enjoy Sabbath. You might want to do some self-assessment here...

- *Anger that stays with you, that settles in your gut, that seethes as resentment
- *Anxiety that becomes chronic at some level and refuses to release its grip
- *Cynicism that indicates you are going through the motions but don't really believe in what you are doing and feel detached if not alienated from others

- *Loss of joy as busyness, stress, fears and doubts become overwhelming and we are drained, sometimes to the point of despair
- *Health problems that result from unaddressed and/or un-processed malaise

I reminded my new friends at this conference that Jesus and his disciples had a fairly busy schedule. And yet he often took them away from the crowds and their incessant claims on him and his crew.

If they needed some R&R—maybe you do, as well. To be a healthy human being, to be at your best, to regain the resilience that has been built into God's amazing design for us.

In Chapter Six of Mark's Gospel, Jesus invites his disciples into a just-in-time, badly-needed Sabbath break. Is inviting you to...

Come away with me
By yourselves
To a quiet place
And get some rest!

Doesn't that sound good?! Hanging out with God, with good friends, with spouse and children and grandchildren, disconnecting from all the harangue, the hullabaloo and the hurry sickness...wow. Sign me up. A command I want to obey!

The Sabbath ordinance, as it turns out, is actually all about encouraging intimacy with God...that restores our sense of well-being, that re-supplies us for the next leg of the adventure. We take all God has to offer us, remember who we are and what we are worth, get clear again about our individual calling, make critical mid-course corrections, know that we are greatly loved anyway, and then return reinvigorated to engage all the drama of real life.

Christ operating behind the headlines, Christ mobilizing us for mission, Christ in the cracks of our over-loaded schedules, Christ underwriting our risks, Christ disarming our fears, Christ fueling our joy, Christ the mediator of all our relationships and arbitrator of all our conflicts, Christ the on-call healer of our wounds. Jesus Christ, our sanctuary, who compels us to center ourselves in Him.

The Challenge

What would it take for you to change your (physically, emotionally, spiritually unhealthy) routine? A diagnosis of diabetes? A stroke? A heart attack? A divorce? An arrest for a DUI? Several friends staging an intervention? I hope not. But maybe it will. And we hope it's not too late.

We all have our blind spots. We can live in stubborn denial. Sabbath is a mandatory time-out, time-away, time-to-reflect-and-correct. The practice of Sabbath is the gift we desperately need, and rarely realize it. Sabbath reminds us that we are not self-made nor self-sufficient, and cannot be entirely self-directed. We are human and contingent and, more than

*we are ready to admit, we are exceedingly vulnerable, who-
ever we are.*

*God knows, God understands and God is prepared to provide
all that we need. Including the revitalizing tonic of rest. Sweet
rest. Not just sleep, but a near-miraculous renewal of body,
soul and spirit by relaxing into the truth about our troubles and
the truth about God's availability and help.*

The Experiment

1. Review the Twelve Steps of Recovery (contemplate their
   biblical roots)
2. Work the Steps with a respected veteran of the recovery
   movement. Before you refuse, please note: I was once
   "kidnapped" by a friend (with years of recovery himself)
   who "forced" me to go through this. I resented it, resisted it (after all, I'm the one who counsels others, I'm
   the teacher, I'm always strong while others are allowed
   to be weak!)—and gained so much from this experience
   that I still review and honor these vital Steps. Whether it is
   alcohol, drugs or some other substance or process addiction ("whoever sins is a slave to sin"...John 8:34) we are all
   hooked on/tripped up by something ("the sin that so easily
   entangles"...Hebrews 12:1).

3. When you get traction—as you retreat from your frustrating, frantic, non-stop, over-burdened life—commit yourself to a regular practice of rest, reflection and renewal in solitude (a Christ-centered version of the Miracle Morning format is one approach) and in the company of friends who are willing to get real and go deep. God shows up when you do.

CHRIST INCOGNITO

No One Saw
This Coming

Nobody expected Jesus to rise from the dead. Nobody.

Not the soldiers who were experts in the art of crucifixion. Nobody survived their brutal executions.

Not the rulers who sentenced him to death. Nobody resisted their will.

Not the empire that controlled the world. Nobody among the elite even noticed.

Not the religious leaders who held him in contempt. They were confident he was gone.

Not his disciples. This was the bitter end of their beautiful movement.

Not the crowds in Jerusalem. Their hopes of a conquering hero were crushed.

Not the principalities and powers, the evil forces in high places, the ministers of hate and cruelty, that conspired to kill the Son of God.

Only Jesus knew, because he trusted his Father to keep his promise and fulfill his purpose.

It was for the joy of the resurrection coming that he endured the pain, carried our shame, forgave his enemies, and gave his life as a sacrifice for us. Jesus the Christ died and rose again so that everybody who believes in him can be rescued from sin and sadness, will be delivered from death and judgment.

On that melancholy Sunday morning nobody imagined an outcome like this.

But everybody, now, is invited to take the gift that inundates our hearts with an everlasting love and transforms all of life.

Christ Revealed

My goal is that they may be encouraged in
heart and united in love
So that they may have the full riches of
complete understanding
In order that they may know
the mystery of God
namely Christ
In whom are hidden all the treasures
of wisdom and knowledge
For in Christ all the fullness of God
lives in bodily form
And in Christ you have been brought
to completeness
[Colossians 2]

This book is not a theological treatise but it is shot through with rich
theological conviction about the God we meet in the Bible and the
Risen Christ who shows up—bidden or unbidden, recognized or
not—in history and in our world today. What follows is grace beyond
belief and the miracle of restoration beyond our wildest hopes.

What happens after Easter? Is the Christ who is triumphant over death immediately launched on a world tour where he is showered with adulation and honors? Does he take a victory lap culminating in the forced subjugation of Rome? Is he enthroned in front of adoring crowds? Does he lock down his kingdom and punish his enemies? Does he finally escape this cruel, ungrateful world?

According to the Gospel of Luke, he takes a long walk and joins two men on a lonely trek from Jerusalem to an obscure village. They were followers at a distance, and completely disheartened by the brutal events over that fateful weekend. The betrayal, the arrest, the trials at night on trumped up charges, the vicious beatings, the disgrace and torment and inevitable lethality of a crucifixion, the death, the wailing of the women, an unceremonious burial.

They didn't recognize him—how could they, Jesus had been executed!—but allowed this vagabond to walk with them along the way. They were blinded by bitter disappointment and shattering sorrow. An animated conversation ensued as the astonishingly uninformed stranger asked them a number of leading questions.

Here's the Question we should all be asking: Didn't the Risen Christ, the King of Kings and Lord of Lords, have something better to do on the very day of his spectacular victory than to chase down a couple of no-name disciples (Cleopas and the other guy) on the road to nowhere?

Answer: Apparently not. This is his agenda, which is no different than what it has always been. He is often present, if unrecognized, in the company of ordinary people, escorting and guiding men and women into a new understanding of God's previously inconceivable plan, unimagined power and amazing love. Revealing (often gradually, sometimes suddenly) without imposing his messianic secret.

Question: How do people find Christ?

Answer: He finds you. In a "chance" encounter. Do you recognize the Stranger who patiently, unobtrusively, relentlessly tracks you (described by one poet as the Hound of Heaven), to pour out his favor on you? And will you be receptive?

As the story begins in Luke 24, Jesus is absent, certain to be dead, an artifact of history, only a memory now to those who had pinned their hopes on him.

"He was sentenced to death...they crucified him...it is the third day since all of this took place."

Then, suddenly, Jesus is present with them, unrecognized and strangely inarticulate.

He caught up and walked along with them. "What are you discussing together as you walk along?" "Are you the only one visiting Jerusalem who does not know the things that have happened there in these days?" "What things?" he asked. To which they replied, "Jesus of Nazareth was a prophet powerful in word and deed...He was condemned to die on a cross...we had hoped that he was the one who was going to redeem Israel."

But now, Jesus is much more articulate and very self-revealing.

"How slow you are to believe all that the prophets have spoken! Did not the Messiah have to suffer?" Beginning with Moses he explained all that the Scriptures said concerning himself.

As the conversation continues Jesus is very much present but still unrecognizable, revealing transformational truth, and now serving his forlorn followers.

"Stay with us." So he went in and sat at the table with them...He took the bread, gave thanks, broke it, and began to give it to them...

In an instant Jesus is recognized (it's impossible that he is here—yet he is!), revealing his identity, thrilling these disciples, and then disappearing.

Then their eyes were opened and they recognized him..."Were not our hearts burning while he talked with us on the road and opened the Scriptures to us?"

After this slow but sure unveiling, Jesus—their inconspicuous companion—is experienced as someone of enormous consequence. He is their risen Lord. He is alive. He has defeated death. All is forgiven, even the worst we have done, and sin has lost its enchantment. Mercy overrides judgment. Empire is not ultimate. The powers that be are discredited and defanged. Everything changes.

They returned at once to Jerusalem...they found the Eleven and those with them..."It is true! The Lord has risen!"

The disciples—from the least to the most prominent, from the most receptive to the most obstinate—are reawakened and energized. Many pagans, skeptics and unbelievers in an ever-widening circle of interest and soul-stirring conviction will experience the same metamorphosis as the breaking news is broadcast across every border.

Life changes forever when the Good News finally sinks in. When the One who has pursued us is recognized as real and embraced as Christ. This is the mystery solved, the secret out in the open, the unapproachable God come close and getting personal.

As always, we are given a choice. Jesus Christ is the all-sufficient source of new life, full restoration, deep wisdom and endless love. Or, this compelling personality is pure fiction, the captivating story is simply myth, the beautiful name a symbol of wishful thinking run amok. How we react doesn't change the fact, of course. And you should always fact-check.

He remains Christ *Incognito.* Until he shows up. And our eyes are opened.

No eye has seen
No ear has heard
No human mind has conceived
The things God has prepared for those who love Him

This is what we speak
Not in words of human wisdom
But in words taught by the Spirit explaining spiritual realities
Moving beyond mere human judgments
we have the mind of Christ
[I Corinthians 2]

A BRIEF HISTORY OF
Christ Incognito:

SEASON	AWARENESS
BC in the Old Testament	Tabernacle and Temple, Patterns, Promises, Prophecies, Anticipation, Mysterious Presence
Conception and Pregnancy	Mary and Elizabeth
Birth in Bethlehem	Mary, Joseph, local Shepherds + townfolk
Exile in Egypt	Mary, Joseph, Magi from Persia + entourage
Childhood in Nazareth	Mary and Joseph + neighbors
Young Adulthood in Galilee	Mary and Joseph + community
Debut of Public Ministry	John the Baptist + followers + spectators
Launching Public Ministry	12 Disciples + demons + early responders
Public Ministry Begins	Crowds who heard him Those who put their trust in him
Public Ministry Builds	Growing, deepening, dividing, expanding in Israel + Samaria... Sending the 70

SEASON	AWARENESS
Entry, Arrest, Trials, Execution	Jerusalem, Judea and environs
Resurrection + 40 Days	The 11, the Women, 500 Eyewitnesses
Risen Christ present by the HS	Early Church + 3000, Acts of the Apostles, spreading across the Roman Empire
Risen Christ across the Centuries	Mission of Grace and Truth people from all tribes and nations all around the world (2.2 billion believers c. 2020)
Risen Christ Returning	Everyone Everywhere

As if it's possible to capture Christ on a timeline! Christ is present, he is on purpose. He comes in disguise, building the case against our self-centeredness and isolation, in favor of our freedom from the pretense of self-sufficiency. Representing the wealth of God the Father to those who recognize their poverty. Ready and willing to reveal himself and his kind intention to lift us, whatever our need. To establish peace in our hearts and peacemaking as our new profession.

Afterword

The framework of the Bible is a teleological narrative. It is salvation-history—not a compendium of religious thought. It is the story of God's design and sustaining involvement in creation, God's purpose as God interacts and intervenes in human affairs, and God's ultimate interest in restoring a universe ravaged by rebellion.

According to the bold reflections of the New Testament writers (and the intimations of Old Testament prophets) on this unfolding cosmic drama, the coming of Christ is the climactic moment in the sacred story. But the participation of Christ with God is traced from the very beginning.

Remember that the Bible was only supposed to be four chapters long—Genesis 1 and 2 followed by Revelation 21 and 22, a seamless, congruent whole. God's grand intentions are clearly revealed in this horizon-to-horizon overview. But something happened. Something cataclysmic. Something sinister and destructive.

From Genesis 3 on, an impossible dilemma presents itself. Humankind goes off the rails, runs away, determines to plot their own course. We may not have been there, but we know the drill. And made it our own.

"Has God really said...?" We've taken the bait and dived deep down into doubt and disarray—after a brief but exhilarating flight into autonomy, clamoring for the sovereignty of the self.

"You shall be as gods!" we were told. And we believed it, were intoxicated by the prospects, until it all fell apart. Until reality set in. The wages of sin, it's called. Death, separation from God, alienation and disintegration on every level, even before the death of the body. A crisis looming that we have yet to solve, even with our best and bravest efforts.

Thus, Christ. The necessity of Love acting on behalf of the God who refuses to quit on the Project. A project that will take millennia to finish.

"In the fullness of time..." Christ makes his appearance into a world at war—a war of all against all. And it's a dark Roman-dominated world. And he's a Jew, subsisting at the edge of the empire. Poor. From a backwater town. Homeless. Exiled, a refugee. Preparing for a lifetime of suffering, opposition, threats, with a cruciform shadow always looming. In other words, Christ Incognito.

Imagine! The One True Living God in love with this fractured and fragmented world. In love with you. With your neighbor. With the stranger. With your enemies. Just imagine.

Imagine! The Creator mingling with men and women who often overlooked him, underestimated him, underappreciated him, and forged a conspiracy to eliminate him. And yet, even stripped and beaten and hung on a cross to die, he kept professing his love, proclaiming forgiveness, predicting a victory over death—to benefit us. Imagine, if you can.

Imagine! The Son becoming human, living among the least and the lonely and the lost, inviting us into the home of our Abba (the too-familiar Hebrew equivalent of Dad—or "Daddy!" as exclaimed by a small child jumping into his father's arms) introducing us to each other as beloved brothers and sisters, promising us an inheritance that is fit for royalty and offering us all the rights and privileges of belonging to God's forever family.

Free your mind to imagine. Then open your heart to encounter him. Abandon your inhibitions and embrace him. Trust him for all he is worth and with all that you have. As you do, you will begin to embody his love, a liberating love the world needs to see, hear, taste, touch, inhale the sweet fragrance of, and believe in. As Christ becomes tangible and accessible, as he emboldens us to represent his incomparable love, without hypocrisy, the glory of our Savior and King will no longer be incognito.

> The one who was from the beginning
> The one we have seen with our eyes
> The one we have looked at
> The one our hands have touched
> This we proclaim concerning the Word of life
>
> The life appeared, we have seen it and testify to it
> We proclaim to you the eternal life
> The one who was with the Father and has appeared to us
> We proclaim to you what we have seen and heard
> So that you also may have community with us
> Our community is with the Father
> and with his Son, Jesus Christ
> We write this to make our joy complete
> [I John 1]

Someone can be seen while they are still at a distance, a safe distance. He must come closer so that he can be heard. He will have to come very close, within our reach, so we can touch him. This is an escalation of intimacy.

If he can be touched, he becomes unmistakably real and, at the same time, extremely vulnerable. If he can be touched, he might get hurt. If he is close enough to touch, he can be gravely wounded, even crucified.

Unconditional love, God's version of love, the highest vision of love, takes the risk and is willing to pay the ultimate price. God the Father, Son and Spirit decided before time began that we are worth it to God. Christ's sacrifice is conclusive proof. His resurrection is the final confirmation—releasing you and me to personally and practically flesh out the love of Christ within the sight and hearing and reach of a waiting, watching and wondering world.

My hope is that...

Imagination becomes wise discernment
We begin to see him, come to know him, pay attention to the work he is doing, start to grasp the significance of his surprising presence

Encounter becomes deep relationship
We want to shed our insecurities, love well, trust implicitly, learn more, become like our Lord

Embrace becomes radical discipleship

We will not hesitate to go where he sends, do what he asks, and invest ourselves wholeheartedly

Embodying the Love of Christ becomes the call, the mission, the way we live

We study this, practice this, take risks for this, partner for this, become this, excel at this, and celebrate the Love of Christ constantly

Christ incognito becomes Christ our everyday companion,

Christ our death-defying, fear-defeating champion, Christ our one certain cornerstone. Becomes Christ made manifest, made plain, made glorious...eye-catching and compelling...Spirit-releasing in the life-giving presence of Christ-followers who authenticate his love.

This is the opportunity of a lifetime. If you have seen him, even if you have caught a tantalizing glimpse, pursue him. Continue Christward and you will certainly come to love and trust him. And discover that he has been searching for you, waiting for you, never as far away as you might have thought.

Ready to welcome you into his multiethnic, intercultural, cross-generational family. To celebrate your return to your true home. Pleased to arm you with his love, energize you with his joy, strengthen you with a hope that will always overcome...so that you can wage peace, spread love, radiate joy and exude hope in a world that has lost its way and forgotten our reason for being.

The modest, unimposing Jesus, almost coy in his incognito presence, makes this outrageous claim when the moment is right—after he has made the case and confirmed his credentials: *I am the Way, the Truth and the Life...no one comes to the Father except through me.* This is beyond bold. Said sincerely by the one who stood as a paragon of sanity, who personified integrity, whose unprecedented powers were only and always used to benefit others.

Is this arrogance? Look at his life. Is this overreach? Is there anyone else like him? Any real rivals to his character, wisdom, moral authority, accomplishments, sacrificial love, influence and inspiration across all of recorded history? This, despite the institutional misrepresentations and/or self-centered agendas that incline us to deflect his appeal.

This is the man who loved tenderly and fiercely, who loved deeply and widely, who spoke simply and profoundly, who healed the weak and confronted the proud...who gave his life willingly, who forgave his tormentors, who predicted his victory over death and came back after three days in the tomb to vindicate his triumph over fear, evil, judgment and death. Who impressed a cowardly cohort of defeated and demoralized men and women to rise to the occasion, to unify around his cause, to give their lives for his impossible mission—the salvation of the whole world.

This is exclusivity without exclusion. Jesus offers what everyone needs, what we are all looking for. Offering what no one else does or can—but offers it to everyone. "Come to me, all of you who are weary, who are worn down, who are overwhelmed by burdens, and I will give you rest."

Offers it freely, extravagantly, and at the same time commands our wholehearted devotion. "Follow me!" When we do, whoever we are, wherever we are coming from, we find that he has come to give us life, life that is full and flourishing, life that never ends. Life enlightened by the Word of God, infused by the Spirit of God, in company with the Son of God...in contrast to the ruinous compulsions (internal and external) that shatter our dreams and crush our hopes.

At the end of a book written by a Christian author there is typically an invitation to "pray the prayer." To invite Christ into your heart. I'm for that. But this is not a How-To book. This is a Who-For book.

This is all about him, about Christ, and all for him. It's also a book about you. You are Who I have in mind. And that You is also plural—it's about Us. We're in this together—with Him.

And, finally, how could it not be about All of Them—which is All of Us (because there is no Us VS Them any longer)—beautiful, talented, broken and bloodied, living on an exceedingly blessed, frighteningly fragile planet that is convulsing from a convergence of crises that provoke a cry for relief, for rescue, for renewal.

Follow Jesus, who is the Christ. That's it. Follow faith-fully. As in...*I believe! Help my unbelief!* Nevertheless, keep moving with him. That's all. That's his call.

No doubt his first followers wanted more information—details, itineraries, schedules, projections, etc. It turns out he only provides it on a need-to-know basis. Along the way. There are mysteries, there are roadblocks, there are unexpected breakthroughs, and times of (productive, not passive) waiting. There is always enough love. There is always a larger purpose, even if it eludes us.

What he wants is your trust. Your total trust. As in the closest of relationships. If you knew all about this journey in advance, you wouldn't go. It's more challenging than you would anticipate and immensely more joyful—more meaningful, more fulfilling—than you could ever imagine. Who else offers that?!

Bibliography

Brooks, David. *The Second Mountain: The Quest for a Moral Life.* Random Books, 2019.

Burke, John. *No Perfect People Allowed: Creating a Come as You Are Culture in the Church.* Zondervan, 2005.

Cahill, Thomas. *Desire of the Everlasting Hills: The World Before and After Jesus.* Doubleday/Random House, 1999.

Chan, Francis. *Crazy Love: Overwhelmed by a Relentless God.* David C. Cook, 2008.

Chan, Francis. *Letters to the Church.* David C. Cook, 2018.

Collins, Francis. *Belief: Readings on the Reason for Faith.* HarperOne, 2010.

Enns, Gaylord. *Love Revolution: Rediscovering the Lost Command of Jesus.* Love Revolution Press, 2018.

Goff, Bob. *Everybody Always: Becoming Love in a World Full of Setbacks and Difficult People.* Thomas Nelson, 2018.

Holland, Tom. *Dominion: How the Christian Revolution Remade the World.* Basic Books, 2019.

Huckins, Jon and Swigart, Jer. *Mending the Divides: Creative Love in a Conflicted World.* InterVarsity, 2017.

Hunter, George. *The Celtic Way of Evangelism: How Christianity Can Reach the West Again.* Abingdon, 2010.

Keller, Timothy. *Counterfeit Gods: The Empty Promises of Money, Sex and Power, and the Only Hope that Matters.* Viking, 2009.

Keller, Timothy. *King's Cross: The Story of the World in the Life of Jesus.* Hodder & Stoughton, 2013.

Keller, Timothy. *The Reason for God: Belief in an Age of Skepticism.* Penguin, 2008.

Koukl, Gregory. *The Story of Reality: How the World Began, How It Ends, and Everything Important that Happens in Between.* Zondervan, 2017.

Labberton, Mark. *The Dangerous Act of Worship: Living God's Call to Justice.* InterVarsity, 2012

Lewis, C. S. *The Great Divorce.* Geoffrey Bles, 1945.

Lyons, Gabe. *The Next Christians: Seven Ways You Can Live the Gospel and Restore the World.* Multnomah, 2012.

Manning, Brennan. *Abba's Child: The Cry of the Heart for Intimate Belonging.* NavPress, 2002.

McLaughlin, Rebecca. *Confronting Christianity: 12 Hard Questions for the World's Largest Religion.* Crossway, 2019.

McManus, Erwin Rafael. *The Barbarian Way: Unleash the Untamed Faith Within.* Thomas Nelson, 2005.

Miller, Donald. *Searching for God Knows What.* Thomas Nelson, 2010.

Moore, Lecrae. *Unashamed.* B&H Publishing, 2016.

Mother Teresa. *Love: A Fruit Always in Season.* Ignatius, 1987.

Muggeridge, Malcom. *Jesus: The Man Who Lives.* HarperCollins, 1984.

Newbigin, Lesslie. *The Gospel in a Pluralist Society.* Eerdmans, 1989.

Nouwen, Henri. *The Return of the Prodigal Son: A Story of Homecoming.* Penguin Random House, 1992.

Platt, David. *Radical: Taking Back Your Faith from the American Dream.* Multnomah, 2010.

Rutledge, Fleming. *The Crucifixion: Understanding the Death of Jesus Christ.* Eerdmans, 2017.

Smedes, Lewis. *Love Within Limits: Realizing Selfless Love in a Selfish World.* Eerdmans, 1989.

Tizon, Al. *Whole and Reconciled: Gospel, Church and Mission in a Fractured World.* Baker, 2018.

Wright, N. T. *Simply Jesus: A New Vision of Who He Was, What He Did, and Why He Matters.* HarperOne, 2018.

Yancey, Philip. *The Jesus I Never Knew.* Zondervan, 2002.

Made in the USA
Columbia, SC
27 December 2019